2ND EDITION

Got a Drop of OIL?

A REFERENCE & PRICE GUIDE TO SMALL OILERS

BY
David J. Moncrief

PUBLISHED BY
L-W BOOK SALES
PO Box 69
Gas City, IN 46933

ISBN#: 0-89538-119-2

Published by: L-W Book Sales
                PO Box 69
                Gas City, IN 46933

Please write L-W Books for our free catalog
of books on Antiques and Collectibles.

Printed in the U.S.A.

Dedication

I am first dedicating this new 2nd Edition of "GOT A DROP OF OIL?" to the two people most important to me, who deserve a lot of the credit for allowing this book to get published: my loyal wife Sherry of 17 years now, who has managed to somehow juggle a full-time professional career, help raise a wonderful son, attend his soccer, basketball, and baseball games (score-keeper too!), Taekwondo, AND keep me in line! . . . and to our wonderful 10 year old son Tyler, who keeps me amazed constantly with the things he has accomplished (a Black-Belt in Taekwondo by age 9!) thus far, and the ease with which he learns things that I never knew about at that young age. They, more than anyone else have put up with me being on the phone at late hours, gathering documentation, being behind the camera for long periods, cleaning cans, and being the first one every day to the mail-box to see what treasures have arrived. Without their assistance and support I might have been much longer seeing this 2nd book finished.

Secondly, for this 2nd Edition, I must once again give very generous credit to my special long-distance friend and fellow collector, Norm Pennie. Without his enduring my hour long phone calls, relentless picking of his mind to glean information on scarce oilers, and borrowing enumerable quantities of oilers from his collection for inclusion in this book, I seriously wonder if it would have made it to publication this year! Norm has many years of experience and a vast knowledge in several areas of collectibles, which has been so valuable in the formation of this edition. Norm's collaboration was the utmost beneficial, and I dare say . . . a necessity! You might say Norm is a walking encyclopedia of Petroliana! I look forward to the day we can meet in person . . . maybe you have already?

Lastly, I'd like to dedicate this 2nd Edition to all of the veteran oiler collectors that have shared their new finds or rare treasures with the rest of us, and to the newer collectors that may have less than 100 pieces in their collection, who are still thrilled by finding more common pieces. All of these folks have also been a huge factor in the completion of this 2nd Edition.

Acknowledgements

As in my 1st Edition, many fine collectors and dealers across the U.S. and Canada played an important and vital role in helping this book materialize. Without them taking a big chance, by sending oilers from their collections long distance for me to photograph, this book might not be bringing you all different pieces than seen in the 1st Edition. This book contains 1,282 photographs (between covers), of which 1,231 are different pieces pictured! I hope that you as a collector will appreciate the opportunity these contributors have afforded all of us to see a lot of pieces that you just don't see or find too often. Some of these loaned pieces are "common", some are "semi-scarce", while others are simply "extremely scarce." Their trust and willingness to help put together this 2nd Edition has been nothing less than amazing. Pieces loaned to me for inclusion in this book total up to an incredible 976!

These fellow collectors that have shared their interesting pieces, documentation, and input are listed in the "DIRECTORY OF CONTRIBUTORS". I wish to let them all know how very, very much they are appreciated for all of their help, whatever form it came in.

It has been left up to each individual contributor as to how they are listed in the directory, according to how, and if they prefer to be contacted. If you make inquiries through the mail with any of these people, it would be a good idea to include a SASE for first time dealings or responses.

I would also like to express a special thanks once again to my very good friends Cheryl and Wayne Koenig for always supporting me, even when an idea for the book might not have sounded feasible. Wayne remains a plentiful wealth of information on Petroliana collectibles and a mentor to me through the years. I value his input and advise whenever available. Thanks for your continued support!

Others that have been immensely helpful in the formation of this edition are: Kerm Lusk for his unwavering trust, generosity, and wonderful contributions – sent over and over; Lawson Veasey for his outstanding effort traveling out of his way, again, to supply huge amounts of needed material for this book; Dick Ekstrand for his enthusiasm in the "sport" of chasing oilers, and his willingness to share latest finds with us all; Jim Miller for his repeated welcome contributions – each box load yielded new surprises; Myron and Scott Schwinn, a father/son collecting team, sending many unique additions for the book; Bill Blair for his seemingly endless source of information, documentation, and desire to educate fellow collectors; Doug Tozer for scarce documentation of rare oilers, and seldom seen oiler displays – nothing short of . . . wow!; Dave Johnson for taking that "leap of faith" across the miles, with many terrific examples loaned; and Mark Maxwell with a seemingly endless variety of wonderful oilers loaned. These are just a few of the larger contributors, though many more fine collectors contributed in many ways. Please see the "DIRECTORY OF CONTRIBUTORS" for a complete listing of these generous collectors. The overall participation has been almost overwhelming and so very gratifying. This is what makes this venture all worthwhile. My hat goes off to **all** of you!

All photo processing was once again performed by: BEDFORD CAMERA & VIDEO of Rogers, Arkansas. These folks have continued their commitment to supplying me once again with consistent quality for almost six months, the time it roughly required me to photograph the total contents of this book. Their patience and cooperation is greatly appreciated once again!

PLEASE UNDERSTAND THAT THIS BOOK IS PRESENTED AS A REFERENCE AND PRICE **"GUIDE"** ONLY, **NOT A SOURCE TO SET OR ESTABLISH VALUES!** The values contained in this book are not "carved in stone", nor "the final word" . . . they are derived from input from other collectors, buyers, sellers, and myself. To my knowledge, there has been no other text or reference book, dealing with this specific collectible, to draw upon to help determine values for both the 1st and 2nd editions. This collectible is basically still new enough that set values cannot be determined yet . . . there are simply too many variables involved to lock-in a predetermined value. What we are providing you with is simply a "direction" to go when trying to arrive at a value for any given oiler. The author and publisher assumes no responsibility for any losses incurred by individuals attempting to buy/sell/trade oilers based upon information found in this book.

Table of Contents

Introduction

You probably used one to lubricate that old single-shot 22-rifle that you grew up with, to keep it working smoothly. Your father used to oil your bicycle with one, so that you could fly like the wind. He likely even uses one to un-stick rusted or frozen nuts and bolts even today. I'll even bet that your mother has had occasions to squirt a few drops of oil on the old oscillating floor fan, making it run quieter, before your old house got air-conditioning. Let's not forget your grandfather and his father . . . what kind of things did they need only a drop or two of some kind of oil for? A typewriter? Their old squeaky automobile? That stubborn lock? Grandma's treadle sewing machine? Did it keep the old Victrola entertaining for generations? How about the old wringer washing machine? What was used on that ancient buggy or carriage hubs and wheels?

All of these applications had one thing in common. . . they utilized some form of a small oiler to dispense drips or drops of some type of oil. It doesn't matter what you call them: handy oilers, oil cans, lubricators, pocket oilers, household oilers, or just plain oilers. Whether they were made of metal, glass, or plastic, people have used small oilers for years upon years for lubricating practically any man-made object that was meant to move.

Small oilers were handy . . . they often were small enough to slip into a car's glove-box, or a pocket, or toolbox . . . thus many were advertised as a "Handy Oiler". Handy oilers of various shapes and sizes have attained a very collectible status, with possibly many thousands yet to be discovered yet by collectors. I personally know of several oiler collectors and collections hovering around 1,000 different pieces. With over 2,000 different pieces amassed by another collector, I can only guess that there is possibly no limit to how many oilers any of us can find, given enough time!

Isn't it great too, that all of us don't like the same oilers? Some like to specialize in only "oil company" brand oilers. Some concentrate on only the old, round, 4oz. design with a 2-way spout, while others like glass bottles of oil every bit as much as a metal handy oiler. Some prefer only lead spouted oilers, and others want only the "oval" shaped cans in their collection. Diversity is the name of this collectible! There seems to be a style of oiler available for every taste!

What about the artwork, graphics, and logo designs found on oilers . . . does this lend to their collectibility? You bet it does! Oilers with attractive graphics, or pictures (also referred to as "picture cans"), are sure to command the most interest, and higher dollar value. I have seen many incredibly gorgeous, graphic oilers in the last three years, that I would consider to be works of art! I for one can't wait to see what unique and scarce oilers surface in the next few years!

About This Book

If you already have the 1st edition of "GOT A DROP OF OIL?" – AN INTRODUCTION & PRICE GUIDE TO SMALL OILERS, you have on hand already a lot of beneficial information that was not duplicated for this book. Sections such as: Cross-Overs, Determining Age, Determining Condition, Determining Value, Pricing, and Cleaning Oilers will not be found in this 2nd edition. I urge you to frequently refer back to the 1st edition for this information, which I feel is still very relevant and necessary to refresh even the experienced oiler collector.

If you are viewing this 2nd edition of "GOT A DROP OF OIL?" for the first time, and do not have the 1st edition, then you are in for a treat! I feel that this 2nd edition makes a great compliment to the 1st edition, as far as showing you more variety, and many more scarce, and extremely scarce oilers. Though values given in the 1st edition are now dated, the oilers pictured and the helpful information included make the 1st book a very useful tool to the oiler collector!

If you need to acquire a copy of the 1st edition to compliment this new 2nd edition, they are still available through the publisher, or myself, the author.

The small oilers that are displayed in this 2nd edition are mostly of the type with spouts, and are squeezed to dispense drops of oil. Exceptions will be glass bottles, (that either take a screw-cap or cork to seal the contents), oilers that apply oil with a rod or stick dipped into the oil, and some with removable tops to facilitate pouring into refillable oilers. Oilers that utilize a vertical "thumb-pump" (railroad type oilers), or a horizontal "trigger-pump" are normally not included, but as with any collectible, there will be one or two exceptions, as evidenced by the "Aladdin's Lamp" style MOBIL oiler for example. Finds like this just have to be shared with all collectors!

Oilers for lubricating purposes shown in this book mostly contained oil for small lubricating jobs, not products that were intended to go into the gas tank or engine of an auto. Other products that were also packaged in the same style containers as the oils, are listed in the category "OTHER PRODUCTS". Many oiler collectors include these other products with the oils, on the same shelf in their collection, as a "go-with" or "go-along". A large majority of the oilers displayed in this book are the type referred to as a "handy oiler". Examples can be seen on the cover.

The primary purpose of this book, as it was with the 1st edition, is to continue to acquaint both the experienced and novice collector with the great diversity available in this collectible. This is not a history of small oilers, nor does this book attempt to show any chronological progression of company name changes or incorporations. An attempt has been made though to arrange oilers of the same brand in a chronological order of age when possible. When known, some dating of pieces has been noted with photos, even if it is just an educated guess.

Note: Underneath the pictures in this book are abbreviations or designations for the sizes and shapes of the oilers. Here are the most common abbreviations and designations used, along with their translations: rnd.=round; oval; obl.=oblong; rect.=rectangular, sq.=square; wide oval; tall obl.=tall oblong, tall rect.=tall rectangular; short rect.=short rectangular; dia.=diameter; wd.=wide; tall.

Also underneath the pictures can be found a combination of: the name of the product, the name of manufacturer or company that sold the product, the name of the country of origin if different than the US, and a price range. Some pictures may also have reference to the original retail price marked on the oiler, and some will show what level of scarcity they are perceived to be. Circa dating of pieces is often noted when known, though most often approximated.

Oilers pictured in this book were photographed with a 35mm camera and close-up lenses to display details to the fullest. If it appears that two items pictured next to each other on a page are nearly identical, refer to the size or capacity stated under each photo. Some look-alike oilers may also only differ by the style or type of spout, different retail pricing marked on the oiler, or different wording of the advertising. Some collectors like to have pieces reflecting every subtle change they can find for a given oiler.

The largest size/capacity oiler shown in this book is generally no larger than a 16oz. size. Many of the metal cans of this size came with a screw-on spout, which qualifies it for inclusion. As with any collectible, there will be some exceptions to cans having spouts.

The "Table of Contents" is divided into alphabetized categories. Within each category oilers are pictured in alphabetical order by usually the most prominent name on the face of the oiler.

What's Out There?

There's the suspicion, the rumor, that a certain brand or company's handy oiler exists . . . will it lead you on a seemingly endless search? It's the thrill of the hunt for that elusive oiler that hardly anyone else has seen, or owns, that keeps us looking and always asking others . . . have you seen one? . . . do you know who has one? . . . was one ever made?

This section was designed for you, the collector. Hopefully it will inspire you to keep the thirst for collecting going strong, and lead you to the thrill of a new discovery!

Have you ever helped dispose of someone's so-called "junk" from their attic, basement, garage, or barn? Don't be so hasty to let it be hauled off to a land-fill or dump, there could be a scarce oiler in one of those tattered boxes! These turn up all the time at yard/garage sales and estate auctions, mixed in with a bunch of miscellaneous items, often sold off for only a few dollars. What brand oiler comes to mind for you when I say "scarce"?

- Does a LION handy oiler really exist? Have you seen one?

- What is the "toughest" handy oiler to find in your opinion . . . or . . . what would you consider to be the "Holy Grail" of all oilers?

- Ever dig out that ancient gun cleaning kit that your grandfather or father used as a young guy? What's in it now?

- How big is a "big" oiler collection?. . . 500 pieces? . . . 1,000? . . . 2,000? Is there a ceiling on how large a collection could grow to?

- Ever hear of a small, round, early, green, TEXACO Sewing Machine oiler?

- How many "different" brands of oilers do you think are out there?

- Have you ever held a real RED INDIAN HOMOIL oiler in your hand? Did you let go of it?

- Does anyone know what the earliest VALVOLINE oiler looks like?

- When was the last time you prowled through your grandfather's barn, attic, or basement? Find any treasures?

- GILMORE dates back a long time, did they have a small oiler?

- How many of you have seen the CONOCO "Minute Man" oiler? Look in this book for one!

- It's green, round, has vertical stripes, has a 2-way spout, it's TEXACO! . . . Is this their earliest oiler?

- How many different variations of the oval GULFOIL oilers are there with the "horse-head"?

- Who owns an EN-AR-CO oval, 3oz., oiler with the "slate-boy" on it? What . . . you didn't know there was one? Check out the one we included in this edition!

- What color is the oldest know AMOCO oiler?. . . Green? Locate the one in the "Oil Company Oilers".

- What does the "oldest" known SHELL oiler look like? Is it in this book?

- It's oval, 3 oz., lead spout, it's PENNZOIL! . . . have you seen one? It exists! I've seen it in a picture.

- How common is a PURITAN oiler with the lion on it?

- UNION is a very old oil company, what does their earliest oiler look like?

- It's round, 1½oz., its a very early QUAKER STATE oiler. See the earliest example we've seen!

- How about an oval, 4oz., lead spout, SOHIO oiler with the outline of Ohio . . . common, or not?

These are questions that have been asked of me by other collectors, and I only can answer but a few. How about you, do some of these questions intrigue, or fuel your collecting and hunting instincts? Many of us suspect that these extremely scarce oilers must exist . . . maybe it's just a matter of time until they surface. Maybe you are already in possession of at least one of them?

Author's Comments

I've been asked where I think this branch of Petroliana collectibles is headed, and for how long will it last? I personally feel that there are still thousands of oilers out there yet to be discovered by you and I, and from the feedback I receive, it appears that this collectible still has quite a future left yet. I see new examples showing up almost monthly that I've never seen before now. I feel that this is one collectible that enables every collector to never duplicate another's collection, with so many variations and brands available. Every collector is almost guaranteed to have his/her own unique and different collection, unlike anyone else's.

Prior to putting out my 1st edition of "GOT A DROP OF OIL?", I hunted the flea markets, antique malls and shops, yard sales, auctions, and developed contacts with other Petroliana collectors to find these oilers, just like many of you do today I'm sure. The drawback to this I feel is that you often are confined to a particular geographic area to search, as I was, since I don't do much long distance traveling. If you are a traveler, and stop at all of the out of town/state shops you come across, you are still limited to finding normally a few pieces at best at any location. Once in awhile you will luck upon the flea market or antique mall that has one booth selling exclusively Petroliana collectibles, and you think that you have found the pot of gold at the end of the rainbow!

While I feel that these sources will always be available for finding some oilers, I have to agree with many of my collector friends that a lot more can be found on the Internet now. I was resistant to buying a home computer in the beginning, and still loved to type on my antique Royal manual typewriter. But, thanks to my wife, she convinced me how much faster I could turn out correspondence and do a whole lot more, faster and more efficiently, with a computer. Once I got my feet wet, I learned about on-line auctions on the Internet. After I got a feel for finding my way around, I discovered another "pot of gold" . . . oilers on auction! It's now about 3 years since my 1st edition came out, and I can personally attest to the never-ending wealth of oilers I've found on the on-line auctions during this period. Yes, there are a lot of the more common oilers offered on auctions, but almost weekly you can find at least one oiler that is at least a little unusual. Not quite as often, you can find oilers offered on auction that rank very high in the desirability and scarcity category. As you might expect though, these oilers also command a lot of interest by bidders, and it's not uncommon to see an extremely scarce oiler go for $100+, $200+, $300+, and even higher! Just remember, oilers that you find out in flea markets, antique malls, and such get somewhat limited viewing by the public, whereas oilers on the Internet auctions are possibly viewed by many thousands of people. Thus, more people are seeing the oilers . . . there's more interest in them . . . bidding wars ensue . . . and higher dollars are sometimes paid for them.

A lot of oiler collectors ask what impact the Internet and on-line auctions have had on this collectible. There are a lot of mixed feelings on this subject! While a lot of collectors have yet to own their first computer and get on-line, there are many more that have become computer savvy, and have found a veritable cornucopia of oilers available through on-line auctions, that they never have seen or only dreamed of before. Almost monthly I have witnessed scarce oilers being put up for auction that I have never seen before! A lot of these seldom seen oilers generate a LOT of interest naturally, and as a result, I often see another identical oiler show up a week or so after the first one is auctioned! Due to the large volume of people on the Internet now, I think that these seldom seen oilers on auction are actually bringing more of the same "out of the woodwork". An owner of a second oiler, like the first one, sees how much interest and dollars this one brought, so maybe he/she wants to see what their oiler will bring . . . thus getting a piece of the pie for themselves! Yes, I feel that the Internet has significantly affected prices on oilers, unfortunately towards the high side, but I still have confidence that fellow collectors will keep prices in reason when buying/selling/trading between themselves . . . off-line! With this said, **I MUST EMPHASIZE THAT THE VALUES SHOWN IN THIS BOOK ARE NOT BASED UPON INTERNET AUCTION PRICES!** I still want this reference book to reflect the buying/selling/trading that is shared between fellow collectors. I enjoy immensely e-mailing on-line friends and fellow collectors, but this takes a back seat to good old one-on-one communication between two collectors, whether it's on the telephone, or at an antiques or oil show!

Fantasy/Reproduction Oilers

Webster's Dictionary defines "Fantasy" as . . . "an unreal image, or illusion". That pretty much sums up what a "reproduced" oiler is, in my estimation. A fantasy, a reproduction, a fake, a copy, a representation, an imitation, or a facsimile . . . it doesn't matter what it's called, a fake is a fake!

Some collectors might not mind creating a "fantasy" piece, or a "representation" of a scarce oiler, just to have an example of it in their collection, in the hopes of some day finding the real thing. This is fine, as long as this copy is not sold to another person, represented as an original! This is where I would like to presume that most of us would draw the line. Fantasy pieces are okay ONLY IF THEY ARE PRESENTED AS SUCH!

I have unfortunately added a few of these reproductions to my own collection over the years, unknown to me at the time I purchased them. After paying a handsome sum for one piece, I did some close inspection of this piece, got in touch with knowledgeable collectors of this brand, and arrived at the terrible realization that I had been duped, as I feel other collectors have unknowingly. Unfortunately, after money and the oiler have exchanged hands, it's often too late to get a refund, especially if purchased over the Internet. I've been confronted with this situation, only to have a seller claim that they never knew that the oiler was not authentic. Hopefully if you find yourself in this type of situation, you will be dealing with a reputable seller that will willingly refund your money and take the piece back. If not, you'll likely be stuck with the fake, and a few less dollars in your pocket, but hopefully a bit wiser to these "to-good-to-be-true" pieces in the future!

Listed on the next page are some descriptions and pictures of oilers that I have both acquired and heard of, that "appear" to be the "real thing", for you to see what a little skill and persistence can produce. These pieces were all represented as "authentic". I must make it clear to you that I am no authority on this subject, but I have enlisted help from collectors of these particular brands to help substantiate, or refute their authenticity. Oddly enough, all of these examples are oil "bottles". I haven't seen a reproduced can yet.

1. **TEXACO HOME LUBRICANT** (see 2 pictures)
    <u>Features:</u> 1¼" dia. x 3⅛" tall clear glass bottle; paper label and seal across cap; plastic screw-cap (NOT bakelite) with fine vertical ribbing; tips of all label corners mitered at 45-degrees; words TEXACO CERTIFIED LUBRICATION on seal are hot-pink color . . . also star in logo at each end; the "**T**" inside logos on seal are yellow color.

    <u>Tips to being fake:</u>   front label . . . identical to mid-1920s oval handy oiler (as seen on cover of 1st edition of "GOT A DROP OF OIL?"); plastic screw-cap . . . should have likely been "bakelite" if a 1920s bottle; paper seal across cap . . . wrong colors; letters shouldn't be hot pink and "**T**" in logos shouldn't be yellow; mitered corners on both labels; this label purported to never been used on a small bottle.

Texaco Home Lubricant

2. **SOHIO COMPLIMENTARY HOUSEHOLD OIL** (see 2 pictures)
    <u>Features:</u> 1½" dia. x 3¾" tall clear glass bottle; paper label and seal across cap; plastic screw-cap (NOT bakelite) with fine vertical ribbing; tips of all label corners mitered at 45-degrees.

    <u>Tips to being fake:</u> plastic screw-cap identical to TEXACO; mitered corners on both labels; this label purported to never been used on a small bottle.

SOHIO Household Oil

3. **GULF HOUSEHOLD OIL** (no picture – this bottle was seen auctioned on the Internet)
    <u>Features:</u> same approximate size glass bottle as TEXACO & SOHIO bottles; paper label and seal across cap; plastic screw-cap with same fine vertical ribbing; tips of all label corners mitered at 45-degrees.

    <u>Tips to being fake:</u> plastic screw-cap identical to TEXACO & SOHIO bottles; mitered corners on both labels; this label purported to never been used on a small bottle.

4. **WINCHESTER "NEW" GUN OIL** (no picture – this bottle was seen auctioned on the Internet)
    <u>Features:</u> same approximate size glass bottle as TEXACO & SOHIO bottles; paper seal across cap; plastic screw-cap with fine vertical ribbing; tips of all label corners mitered at 45-degrees.

    <u>Tips to being fake:</u> plastic screw-cap identical to TEXACO & SOHIO bottles; paper label showing "New" GUN OIL labeling, identical to handy oiler seen on page #73 - photo #6 in the 1st edition of "GOT A DROP OF OIL?"; mitered corners on both labels; this label purported to never been used on a small bottle.

5. **KEEN KUTTER OIL** (no picture – this bottle seen auctioned on the Internet)
   Features: cork-top, round, brown glass bottle . . . about 4"–6" tall; circa: 1930s or earlier; no labeling . . . but brand name was etched across front of bottle; very clean, crisp etching . . . no obvious chips or flaws.

   Tips to being fake: etching of brand name is too crisp and clean; no chips or flaws . . . looked too recent; this bottle purported never to have existed.

6. **WINCHESTER GUN OIL** (see picture)
   Features: 3¼" wide x 1⅞" dp x 7⅜" tall; cork-top, brown glass bottle; circa: late 1800s–1900; no labeling . . . but brand name was etched across front of bottle: very clean, crisp etching . . . no obvious chips or flaws.

   Tips to being fake: etching of brand name is too crisp and clean; no chips or flaws . . . looks too recent; this bottle purported never to have existed.

*Winchester
Gun Oil*

7. **RUSDUN SEWING MACHINE OIL** (see picture)
   Features: 3½ fluid oz., cork-top, clear glass bottle; paper label.

   Tips to being fake: edges of label obviously hand-trimmed when viewed under magnification; tear mark on left side of label . . . NOT a tear . . . label is a color copy of an original.

*Rusdun Sewing
Machine Oil*

PETROLIANA COLLECTOR
Norm Pennie
PO Box 2960
Sumas, WA 98295
Ph: 604/437-5635

**COLLECTOR OF HOUSEHOLD OIL,
LIGHTER FLUID, & GUN OIL TINS**
Kerm Lusk
Ph: day - 330/877-9925   eve - 330/796-1288
email: kjcllusk@aol.com

**COLLECTORS OF OILERS & TIN LITHO
ADVERTISING**
Lawson & Lin Veasey
310 Ladiga St., SE
Jacksonville, AL 36265
Ph: Hm – 256/782-3462
     Wk – 256/782-5650
email: Hm – llv44@msn.com
         Wk – lveasey@jsucc.jsu.edu

PETROLIANA COLLECTORS
Doil & Betty Scruggs
Rogers, AR

**Author of "GOT A DROP OF OIL?"
and OILER COLLECTOR**
David J. Moncrief
4016 Rocky Ridge Trail
Rogers, AR 72756
Ph: 501/631-2811
email: djmoil@aol.com

COLLECTOR OF OILERS, PATCHES & MAPS
C.E. Wells
6533 Monnett Road
Climax, NC 27233
Ph: 336/674-6254

PETROLIANA COLLECTOR
Roger Berta
PO Box 707
Seneca, IL 61360
Ph: 815/357-6447

ANTIQUE TOOLS & TOOL CHESTS
Harvey & Anne Henderson
1717 Rancho Cajon Place
El Cajon, CA 92019
Ph: home - 619/447-4953
     office - 619/588-9727
email: harveyanneh@aol.com

PETROLIANA COLLECTOR
Wayne Koenig
830 Kings Row
Lumberton, TX 77657
Ph: 409/755-2459
email: koenigsite@msn.com

JAMES C. MILLER
42544 Applecreek
Plymouth, MI 48170
Ph: 734/455-0839
email: jimoilcan@aol.com

COLLECTOR – OILERS & SINCLAIR ITEMS
Mark Maxwell
37966 CR 33
Warsaw, OH 43844

SMALL OIL CAN COLLECTOR
Richard A. Ekstrand
2130 Cardinal Drive
Springfield, IL 62704-2206
Ph: 217/546-7733
email: djeilfl@msn.com

TEXACO & IRVING OIL COLLECTOR
Bud Irving
13434 27th Avenue
White Rock, B.C. V4P 1Z1
Canada
Ph: 604/538-0856
email: birving@telus.net

GULF COLLECTOR
Dwaine R. Benson
7621 Barryknoll
Port Arthur, TX 77642

JAMES T. VAUGHAN
4921 Cralles Road
Amelia, VA 23002
Ph: 804/561-3132
email: mvaughan@tds.net

COLLECTOR OF CANADIAN OIL CANS
Ted Appleby
29 Baptiste, Alberta T9S 1R7
Canada

GUN OIL COLLECTOR
Dave Johnson
1701 Silver Creek Circle
Sioux Falls, SD 57106
Ph: 605/361-8187
email: SDakotaDave@cs.com

**OILER COLLECTOR &
GRAPHIC DESIGNER**
Kandi Kinney
Creative Juices, LLC
6205 Crestwood Drive
Alexandria, VA 22312
Ph: 703/750-2012

**DON LOUGHREN
"ALL CANADIAN SERVICE
STATION MUSEUM"**
Regina, Saskatchewan Canada
email: dloughren@cableregina.com

**PENCIL & TUBE OILERS;
HANDY OILERS ALL TYPES**
Myron Schwinn
4330 Blackjack Road
St. George, KS 66535
Ph: 785/494-2487

CANS & STUFF
Scott & Sandra Schwinn
203 S. Pine Street
Westmoreland, KS 66549
Ph: 785/457-3402

**SPECIALIZING IN
LEAD-TOP OILERS**
Ed Weatherly
315 Palo Verde Lane
Prescott, AZ 86301
Ph: 928/445-9205

WINCHESTER COLLECTOR
Fred Geyer
email: kkfilter@twrtc.com

**COLLECTOR OF LIGHTER FLUID
CONTAINERS**
Mike Brennend
email: Mikebrennend@yahoo.com

**SINCLAIR & OLDER
PHILLIPS 66 COLLECTOR**
Gary Humphrey
23 Division Road
Queensbury, NY 12804
Ph: 518/798-4214
email: garylynn@superior.net

TEXACO COLLECTOR
Gary Oelkers
122 Kincardine Drive
Bella Vista, AR 72715
Ph: 501/876-2356
email: gojo@cox-internet.com

RED INDIAN COLLECTOR
Doug Tozer
RR6
Markdale, Ontario N0C 1H0 Canada
Ph: 519/986-2984

GENERAL COLLECTOR
Bill Blair
(Inactive in recent years)
Ph: 905/852-6711

SMALL OILERS, QUARTS, SIGNS
Jim Looby
6058 Lost Creek Drive
Corpus Christy, TX 78413-3840
Ph: 361/980-0620

**HANDY OIL & LIGHTER FLUID
COLLECTOR**
Doug Eyman
2707 Kimberly Road
Lancaster, PA 17603-7007
Ph: 717/397-2597
email: dbnmops@aol.com

B.F. GOODRICH
Multi-Use Oil, Oval, 4oz.,
made in Kitchener, Canada,
(scarce) – **$50-70**

CHRYCO
Manifold Heat Control Valve
Solvent, Rect., 8 oz., Canada
$25-35

CHRYCO
Manifold Heat Control Valve
Pene. Fluid, Rect., 10 Imp.oz.,
Canada, circa 1960s – **$20-30**

CHRYSLER
Lock-Ease
Short Rect., 4 oz.
$20-35

DELCO
Div. of General Motors Corp.,
Special Light Motor Lub. Oil,
Rect., 4 oz. – **$50-75**

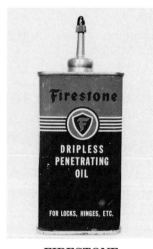

FIRESTONE
Dripless Penetrating Oil,
Rect., 4 oz., large logo
$40-50

FIRESTONE
Dripless Penetrating Oil,
Rect., 4oz.
$35-45

FIRESTONE
4 oz., circa 1940s
$19-29

FIRESTONE
Door-East Dripless Oil,
Rect., 4 oz., Circa 1950s-60s
$25-35

FIRESTONE
Fine Machine Oil, Rect., 4 oz.
$20-27

FORD
Penetrating Fluid, Rect.,
8 oz., Canada
$22-32

GM
Dripless Penetrating Oil, General
Mtrs. Parts Div., Short Rect.,
4 oz., very scarce –**$60-80**

GM
General Use Oil, Oval, 4 oz.,
extremely scarce – **$85+**

GM
RuGlyde Penetrating Rubber
Lubricant, Rect., 8oz.
$30-42

GM
Dripless Penetrating Oil,
Rect., 4 oz.
$50-60

GM
Dripless Oil, Short Rect., 4
oz., Canada, circa 1957
$50-60

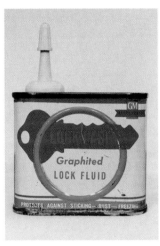

GM
Lock-Ease, Short Rect., 4 oz.,
circa 1950s – **$50-60**

GOODYEAR
General Use Oil, Rect., 4 oz.
$30-45

GOODYEAR
All-Weather General Use Oil,
Rect. 4 oz.
$30-45

GOODYEAR
All-Weather Dripless
Penetrating Oil, Rect., 4 oz.
$30-45

GOODYEAR
Dripless Penetrating Oil,
Rect., 4 oz.
$30-40

GOODYEAR
Dripless Penetrating Oil,
Rect., 4 oz., circa 1950s-60s
$18-29

HARLEY-DAVIDSON
Chain Saver-Fluid Chain
Lubricant, Rect., 8 oz.,
circa 1950s - **$75+**

HUDSON
Dripless Penetrating Oil,
Short Rect., 4 oz., very scarce
$125+

INDIAN
Chain Oil Indian Motorcycle Co.,
1¾" dia. x 3" tall reservoir, paper
label, extremely scarce – **$75+**

INDIAN
Penetrating Oil, Rect., 8 oz.,
circa 1950s, very scarce
$175+

MOPAR
Dripless Penetrating Oil, Rect.,
4 oz., circa 1940s, very scarce
$100+

MOPAR
Speedometer Lubricating Oil,
Oval, 1 oz., circa 1948, scarce
$35-55

MOPAR
Manifold Heat Control Valve
Solvent, Rect., 8 oz.
$16-23

MOPAR
Lock-Ease, Short Rect., 4 oz.
$28-38

MOPAR
Dripless Penetrating Oil,
Obl., 4 oz., paper label
$30-40

NASH
General Use, Rect., 4 oz.,
very scarce
$100+

RED AUTO
General Use Oil, B.F.
Goodrich, Oval, 4 oz.
extremely scarce – **$130-200**

STUDEBAKER – The
Studebaker Corp., Dripless Pene.
Oil, Rect., 4 oz., circa 1940s,
extremely scarce – **$150+**

WILLYS
Willys-Overland Mtrs.,
General Use Oil, Rect., 4 oz.,
very scarce – **$125**

WILLYS
Willys-Overland Mtrs.,
Dripless Penetrating Oil, Rect.,
4 oz., very scarce – **$125+**

Automotive Related Oilers

MACK
Mack Mfg. Corp., Dripless
Penetrating Oil, Rect., 4 oz.,
extremely scarce – **$200+**

Business/Office Related Oilers

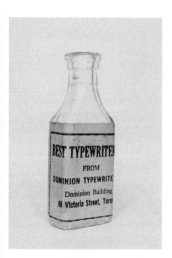

BEST
Typewriter Oil, Dominion
Typewriter Co., 1 oz., Canada
$10-17

CARTER'S
Ideal Typewriter Oil,
Rnd., 2 oz.
$10-19

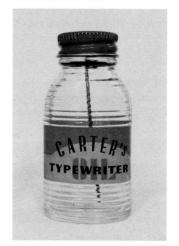

CARTER'S
Typewriter Oil, 2 oz.
$10-19

COMPTOMETER OIL
Felt & Tarrant Mfg. Co.,
1¼" dia. x 4¾" tall with tube
price: 35 cents **$27-35**

FILMO OIL
Bell & Howell Co., For
Camera Only, 1" wd x 1/2" dp
x 33/8" tall, scarce – **$15-25**

FILMO
Bell & Howell Co., For
Camera Only, 13/16" sq. x
25/16" tall, scarce – **$15-25**

FILMO
Bell & Howell Co., Projector
Oil, 1"wd x 9/16"dp x 37/16" tall
$13-20

FILMO
Bell & Howell Co., Projector
Oil, 7/8"sq x 2" tall – **$13-20**

FILMO OIL
Bell & Howell Co., For projector only, 7/8" sq. x 21/2" tall
$13-20

FINEST
Typewriter Oil, The Visible
Writing Machine Co., Rnd.,
1 oz. with box – **$10-18**

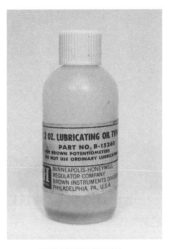

HONEYWELL
Lubricating Oil, Rnd., 2 oz.
$4-6

INVINCIBLE
Typewriter Oil,
11/8" dia. x 21/8" tall
$13-20

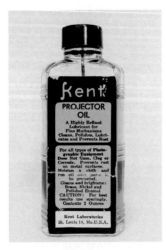

KENT
Projector Oil, Kent
Laboratories, 2 oz.,
circa 1940s-50s – **$7-13**

KODASCOPE
Lubricating Oil, Eastman
Kodak Co., 11/4" dia. x
31/2" tall with box – **$17-23**

L.C. SMITH & CORONA
Typewriter Oil
11/8" dia. x 23/8" tall
$18-22

L.C. SMITH & CORONA
Typewriter Oil,
1" dia. x 25/8" tall
$15-22

LIBERTY
Typewriter Oil,
Liberty Ink Co., Rnd., 2 oz.
$15-22

MASTERGRADE
Typewriter Oil,
Wholesale Typewriter Co.,
1" dia. x 2 1/2" tall – **$10-17**

MORTON'S
Typewriter Oil, Morton Mfg.
Co., 1 5/8" dia. x 4 1/8" tall
$18-25

W.F. NYE
Superior Type Writer Oil,
1 oz., scarce
$17-27

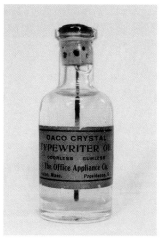

OACO CRYSTAL
Typewriter Oil, The Office
Appliance Co., 1 3/8" dia. x
3 1/2" tall – **$15-22**

The OLIVER
Typewriter Oil, 1 1/8" dia. x 2"
tall with box, price: 20 cents,
very scarce – **$40-55**

RCA
Lubricating Oil for
16mm projectors, 1 oz.
$10-15

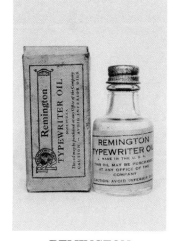

REMINGTON
Typewriter Oil, 1 1/8" dia. x
2 1/4" tall with box
$16-23

ROBINS
Tape & Phono
Drive Oil, 2 oz.
$10-15

SANFORD'S
Household & Typewriter Oil,
Sanford Ink Co., 2 oz.
$17-25

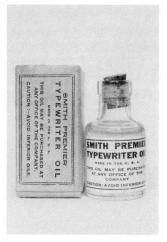

SMITH PREMIER
Typewriter Oil, 1 1/8" dia. x
2 1/16" tall with box, very
scarce – **$28-40**

SPECIAL
Typewriter Oil, Many-Use
Oil Corp., 1" dia. x 2 5/8" tall
$9-16

STAFFORD'S
Lubricator Oil for Typewriters
& All Fine Machines,
1¼" dia. x 3" tall – **$12-18**

**TAYLOR
TYPEWRITER STORE**
Typewriter Oil, 1 oz., scarce
$25-37

TRUE-MARK
Typewriter Oil,
1¼" dia. x 3⅛" tall
$9-18

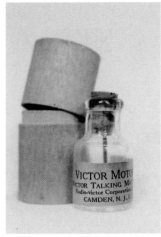

VICTOR MOTOR OIL
Victor Talking Machine Div.
Radio-Victor Corp. of
America, 1" dia. x 11/16" tall
with wood tube, very scarce
$30-40

(The) WEBSTER
Typewriter Oil,
F.S. Webster Co., Rnd., 1 oz.
$10-23

**WESTERN UNION
TELEGRAPH CO.**
Typewriter Oil, Rnd., 2 oz.
$17-26

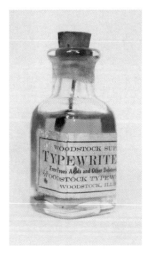

WOODSTOCK
Superior Typewriter Oil,
Woodstock Typewriter Co.,
Woodstock, IL,
1⅛" sq. x 2⅜" tall,
very scarce – **$28-38**

BLACK SHIELD
Watch Oil, Swartchild & Co.,
11/16" sq. x 17/8" tall,
Switzerland – **$10-18**

HAMILTON PML 79 OIL
Hamilton Watch Co., "Made especially for
men's watches" bottle: 5/8" sq. x 17/8" tall,
3.5cc – **$14-20**

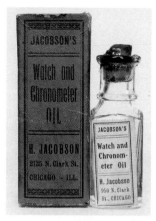

JACOBSON'S
Watch & Chronometer Oil,
13/16" sq. x 21/8" tall with box
$10-20

JENKINS'
Clock Oil, Prepared for E.A.
Cowan & Co., 11/4" dia. x
21/8" tall – **$10-20**

LA PERLE
Clock Oil, Hammel Riglander
Pennant, 13/16" dia. x 31/4"
tall, France – **$14-19**

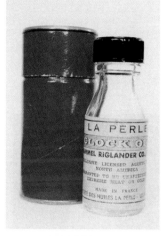

LA PERLE
Clock Oil, Hammel Riglander
Co., 13/16" dia. x 31/8" tall
with tube, France – **$17-22**

MARCO
Watch Oil, C & E Marshall
Co., 1" sq. x 11/4" tall with
box – **$14-20**

LONGINES
Watch Oil, Bottle: 15/8" wd. x 5/8" dp. x 21/8"
tall with 2-pc. box, dated: 5-20-57
$15-22

MOEBIUS
Superior Clock Oil,
H. Mobius & Son,
11/8" dia. x 2" tall – **$15-24**

W.F. NYE INC.
Electric Clock Oil, Rnd.,
1 oz., brown glass
$19-25

PEARL
Clock Oil, Hammel,
Riglander & Co., 1¼" dia. x
3⅜" tall with tube – **$13-16**

(The) R & L OIL
A Superior Watch Oil,
Ranlett & Lowell, Co.,
1" dia. x 1⅝" tall –**$10-18**

SUPERFINE
Watch Oil, W. Cuypers,
1" dia. x 1⅝" tall, Germany
$14-21

V.T.F.
Wrist Watch Oil, 13/16" sq. x
2⅛" tall, price: 35 cents
$13-20

ZENITH
Superior Oil, For American
& English Clocks, 1⅝" sq. x
3¼" tall, England – **$17-27**

ZENITH
Bracelet Oil, Zenith Mfg. &
Chemical Corp., ¾" sq. x
2 5/16" tall – **$8-15**

Cutting/Honing/Tapping Oilers

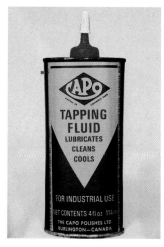

CAPO
Tapping Fluid, The Capo
Polishes Ltd., Oval, 4 oz.,
Canada, "Replicated" – **$18-29**

CENTURY
Threading Fluid, Century
Drill & Tool Co., Rect., 4 oz.
$11-18

COOL TOOL
Cutting & Tapping Fluid,
Monroe Fluid Technology,
Rect., 4 oz. – **$11-18**

HOMART
Pipe Thread Cutting Oil, By
Sears, Roebuck & Co., Rect.,
8 oz. – **$10-18**

HOMART
Pipe Thread Cutting Oil, By
Sears, Roebuck & Co., Rect.,
8 oz. – **$10-18**

KA-BAR
Honing Oil, Rect., 4 oz.
$25-35

MISTIC METAL MOVER
A Cutting Fluid, Rnd., 4 oz.,
paper label – **$14-22**

MOLY-DEE
Tapping Fluid, Arthur C.
Withrow Co., Tall rect., 4 oz.,
circa 1963-73 – **$17-26**

MOLY-DEE
Tapping Fluid, Rect., 4 oz.
$15-24

NORTON OIL
(Formerly PIKE OIL), Rect.,
4 oz., price: $1.49,
circa 1963-73 – **$17-24**

NORTON
Sharpening Stone Oil, tall,
Rect., 4 1/2 oz.
$8-14

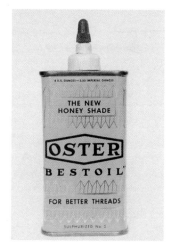

OSTER BESTOIL
For Better Threads,
Rect., 4 oz.
$13-22

PIKE'S STONOIL
For Oilstones, 6 oz.,
very scarce, (front view)
$90+

PIKE'S STONOIL
(close-up view)

PIKE OIL
Behr-Manning, The Best
for Oilstones, Oval, 3 oz.,
semi-scarce – **$56-77**

PIKE OIL
Behr-Manning Corp.,
Sharpening-Lubricating,
Oval, 3 oz. – **$22-33**

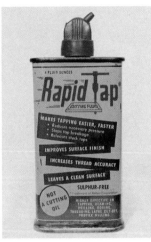

RAPID TAP
Cutting Fluid, Rect., 4 oz.,
circa 1963-73
$11-18

RELTON
A-9 Aluminum Cutting
Fluid, Rect. 4 oz.
$11-17

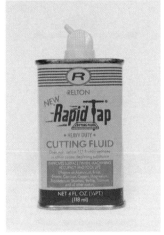

RELTON RAPID TAP
Heavy Duty Cutting Fluid,
Rect., 4 oz.
$11-16

RIDGOIL
Cutting Oil, The Ridge Tool
Co., Oval, 4 oz.
$15-24

RUSSELL'S
Honing & Sharpening Oil,
Rect., 4 oz.
$10-15

STUART'S THRED KUT
Cutting Oil, D.A. Stuart Oil
Co., Rect., 16 oz., Pat'd 1926
$17-26

TAP MAGIC
Not a Cutting Oil,
Rect., 4 oz.
$10-20

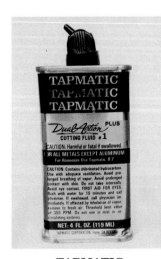

TAPMATIC
Cutting Fluid, Rect., 4 oz.,
circa 1963-73
$10-16

Cutting/Honing/Tapping Oilers

WULFF
Honing Oil, 16 oz.
$13-20

General Use Oilers

AERO
Machine Oil, Boyle-Midway
(Canada) Ltd., Obl., 3 oz.
$22-32

ALLIED
Machine Oil, Allied Drug
Products Co., Obl., 3 oz.
$14-24

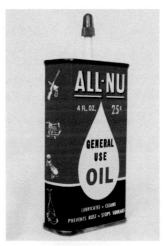

ALL-NU
General Use Oil, Rect. 4oz.
$16-26

AMERICAN
Dripless Oil, American
Grease Stick Co., Rect., 4 oz.,
price: 39 cents – **$15-24**

A-M-R
Handy Oil, A-M-R Chemical
Co., Inc., Rect. 4 oz.
$17-27

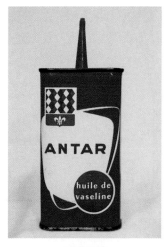

ANTAR
Huile de Vaseline,
Rect., 4 oz., France
$25-35

APPROVED PRODUCTS
Machine Oil, 3 oz.,
copyright 1938
$12-19

ARAL
Allzweck Ol, Rect., 4 oz.,
with bar-code, Germany
$19-30

ARROW
Machine Oil, Arrow
Petroleum Co., Oval, 3 oz.
$20-30

ATLANTIC OEL
Oval, 150 ccm (about 5 oz.)
Germany, (front view)
$50-65

ATLANTIC OEL
(close-up view)

ATLANTIC OIL
Oval, 125 ccm (4 oz.),
Germany
$40-60

BALKAMP
Dripless Oil, Napa, Short,
Rect., 4 oz., circa 1963-73
$15-25

BEAR
Household Oil (Formerly
PIKE OIL), oval, 3 oz.
$21-29

BERRYMAN E-Z DOZ-IT
Penetrating Oil, Rect., 8 oz.
$8-16

BEST
Machine Oil,
Lustrwax Company, 4 oz.
$8-14

GENERAL USE OILERS

B-K PENETRANT
B-K Service Products,
Oval, 4 oz., circa 1950s-60s
$17-25

B-K PENETRANT
Rect., 4 oz.
$15-22

B-K LUB-A-SPRAY
Rnd., 1/2 oz.
$5-10

BLUE RIBBON
Penetrating Oil, International
Metal Polish Co., Inc., Oval,
3 oz., paper label – **$30-40**

BLUE RIBBON
Lubricating Oil, Oval, 4 oz.
$15-24

BLUE RIBBON
Heavy Grade "A" Lubricating
Oil, Hub States Corp., Rect.,
8 oz., circa 1963-73 – **$12-21**

BLUE SEAL
Household Oil, Illinois Farm
Supply Co., Rect., 4 oz.,
scarce – **$35-50**

BONDED
Fine Household Oil,
Rect., 4 oz.
$13-21

BOT LUBE
Farnum Companies, Rect.,
4 oz., circa 1963-73
$13-20

BUDGET
All Purpose Oil, Oval, 4 oz.,
England/Canada
$35-45

BUSTER BROWN
Machine Oil, Rigo Mfg. Co.,
2 oz. – **$18-28**

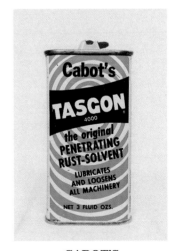

CABOT'S
Tasgon, Penetrating Rust-
Solvent, Obl., 3 oz.
$13-20

27

CABOT'S
Lubri-Tasgon, Penetrating
Lubricant, Obl., 3 oz.
$13-20

CAPO
Stainless Machine Oil, The
Capo Polishes Ltd., 3 oz.,
Canada – **$12-20**

CAPO
Rust-Off Penetrating Oil,
Oval, 4 oz., Canada
$20-29

CAPO
Stainless Lubricating Oil,
Oval, 4 oz., Canada,
"Replicated" – **$22-29**

CARBONA
Pin Point Oiler, Rnd., 1/3 oz.
$11-17

CASTROL
Huilit, Rect., 4 oz., France
$25-35

**COAST TO COAST
STORES**
3" dia. x 7¼" tall
$35-50

COMMERCE
Machine Oil, Commerce
Petroleum Co., Oval, 3 oz., very
scarce (front view) –**$40-55**

COMMERCE
Machine Oil, (back view)

CORO
Lubricating Oil, The Coro Oil
& Rubber Co., Ltd., Wide Oval,
7½ oz., England –**$40-52**

CRAFTSMAN
Lubricating Oil, By Sears,
Roebuck & Co., Rnd., 8 oz.
$14-24

CRESSY'S
Machine Oil, John R. Cressy
Co., 4 oz., brown glass,
Canada – **$25-35**

CROWN
Penetrating & Cleaning Oil,
Rect. 4¹/2 oz., circa 1963-73
$16-26

DE LAVAL OIL
The De Laval Separator Co.,
Triangular shape x 3¹/4" tall, very
scarce, paper label – **$38-50**

DISSOPLAST
Super Degrippant, Rect.,
4 oz., France
$22-30

DIXON'S
Graphited Oil, Joseph Dixon
Crucible Co., Oval, 3oz.
$28-36

DIXON
Graphite Oil, Oval, 3 oz.
$12-22

DIXON'S
Lubricating Graphite,
1/2" dia. x 5" long
$9-14

DRI SLIDE
Dry Film Lubricant,
Rect., 8 oz.
$11-15

DRI SLIDE
Moly Dry Film Lubricant,
Rect., 4 oz.
$13-20

DRITZ
All-Purpose Oil, Scovill,
Rect., 4 oz., price: $1.25,
circa 1963-73 – **$13-18**

DUTCH BRAND
General-Use Oil, Van Cleef
Bros., Oval, 4 oz., paper
label, very scarce – **$58-75**

EDISON
Oil, T.A. Edison, Inc., 1¹/4"
dia. x 4³/4" tall, very scarce
$26-35

EDISON
Diamond Oil, T.A. Edison, Inc.,
1¹/4" wd. x ³/4" dp. x 3¹/16" tall,
very scarce – **$20-28**

EDJOL
Machine Oil,
J.E.T. Pharmacal Co., 3 oz.
$5-10

ELEGANT
Handy Oil, Elegant Products
Ltd., Oval, 4 oz., Canada,
"Replicated" – **$18-28**

EVER-BEST
Household Oil, Hardware
Associates, Inc., 4 oz.
$12-18

EVER-READY
Machine Oil, The
Ever-Ready Co., Oval, 4 oz.
$28-40

EVER-READY
Machine Oil, Ever-Ready
Co., Div. of Plough, Inc.,
Oval, 4 oz. – **$24-32**

EVER-READY
Oil, Obl., 2 oz.
$18-28

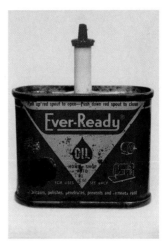

EVER-READY
Oil, Obl., 1 oz.
$11-15

EVER-READY
Oil, Obl., 1 oz.
$9-12

EXCELENE
Lubricating Oil, The Humber
Oil Co., Ltd., Wide Oval, 7½ oz.,
England, very scarce – **$75+**

EXCELENE
Lubricating Oil, The Humber
Oil Co., Short Oval, 4 oz.,
England, very scarce – **$45-70**

EXCELENE
Lubricating Oil, Wide Oval,
7½ oz., England, scarce
$38-52

EXTRA
Machine Oil, Put up by: G.C.
Taylor – Propr. of "Taylor's
Oil of Life", 3oz. – **$8-15**

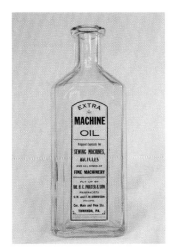

EXTRA
Machine Oil, Put up by: Dr.
H.C. Porter & Son, 6 oz.
$12-19

FAIRWAY
Oil, Obl., 3 oz.
$14-22

FAMILEX
Machine Oil, Rect., 6 oz. –
25 cents, Canada
$40-55

FAMILEX
Machine Oil, Rect.,
6 oz., Canada
$30-45

**FARMERS UNION
CO-OPERATIVE**
3" dia. x 7" tall
$30-40

FARMERS PRIDE
High Grade Oil, Put up by:
Hulman & Co., Oval, 4 oz.,
very scarce – **$90+**

FLAM
White Oil, Rect., 4 oz.,
Belgium – **$30-38**

FLARE
Handy Oil, Rnd., 4 oz.
$13-20

(George) FOSTER'S
Jim Dandy, "The Oil of 100
Uses", George Foster Inc., 8 oz.
$12-17

4-WAY OIL
Old Gold Chemical Co.,
Oval, 3 oz.
$20-30

FRENCH'S
Machine Oil, The R.T.
French Co., 3 oz.
$30-50

GEM
Machine Oil, Mfd. By Frank
Miller & Sons, 2 oz., scarce
$16-25

GENERAL
Utility Oil,
The Koline Co., 3 oz.
$22-30

GLADSTONE
Heavy Paraffine Oil,
Rnd., 2 oz. – no label
$12-17

GOLD CREST
Fine Parts Oil, Sears,
Roebuck & Co., Oval, 4 oz.,
scarce – **$60-70**

GOLDEN
Household Oil, Illinois Oil
Co., Rnd., 8oz., price: 25 cents,
circa 1930s – **$20-30**

GRANTS
Machine Oil, W.T. Grant Co.,
6 oz. – **$13-20**

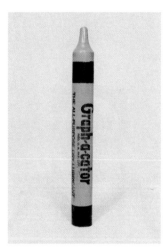

GRAPH-A-CATOR
The All-Purpose Dry
Lubricant, Rnd., 1/3 oz.
$4-9

GRAPHOL
Graphite Rust Solvent &
Preventative, Rnd., 8 oz.,
England – **$20-25**

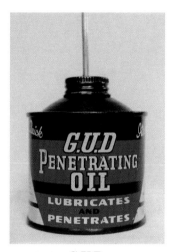

G.U.D.
Penetrating Oil, Rnd.,
6 oz., New Zealand
$24-30

HANDY OIL
Great Easter Oil Co.,
Rnd., 4 oz.
$27-37

HAWES
Machine Oil, 6 oz.
$17-25

HAWES
Machine Oil, Oval, 4 oz.,
Canada, "Replicated"
$18-28

HOME OIL
Oiler, 21/8" dia. x 41/4" tall
$16-26

32

HOME OIL
Buffalo Specialty Company,
2⁷/₈ oz. with box, (front view)
$18-25

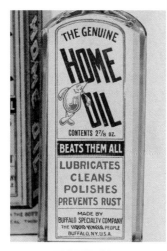

HOME OIL
(Close-up view)

HOME OIL
3¹/₂ oz. with box
$18-25

IDEAL
Utility Oil, Universal
Chemical Co., Rect., 4 oz.,
circa 1940s – **$40-50**

IDEAL
Premium Household Oil,
R.M. Hollingshead Co., Rect.,
4 oz., 35 cents – **$14-20**

IDEAL
Super Penetrating Oil,
Classic Chemical Co., Rect.,
4 oz., circa 1973-on – **$13-20**

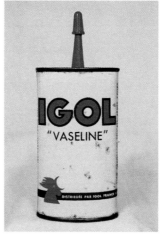

IGOL
"Vaseline", Oval,
3 oz., France
$23-33

INDIAN
Household Oil, Devil
Laboratories, Oval, 4¹/₂ oz.,
very scarce – **$150+**

INTERNATIONAL
Penetrating Oil,
Tall, Rect., 4 oz.
$16-25

JEAP JUICE
Oval, 3oz., paper label,
"Complimentary"
$30-40

JENNY
Solvenized Household Oil,
Jenny Mfg. Co., Rect., 4 oz.
$14-24

J.S.H. & CO.
3" dia. x 7" tall
$25-35

KANT-RUST Penetrating
Graphite Lubricant, 3" dia. x
5" tall reservoir, circa late
1920s-early 1930s – **$35-45**

KANT-RUST
Graphite Lubricant, Oval,
3 oz., circa 1920s-30s,
extremely scarce – **$70+**

KANT-RUST
Penetrating Graphite
Lubricant, Oval, 3 oz.,
circa 1930s – **$35-55**

KANT-RUST/3-IN-1
Penetrating Graphite Lubricant,
Boyle-Midway, Inc., Obl., 3 oz.,
circa late 1950s – **$25-35**

KAYO
Oil, Fairview Chemical Co.,
Tall, Rect., 8 oz., circa early
1930s, scarce – **$70+**

K-B
Mineral Sperm Oil, The
Kunz Oil Co., Rnd., 4 oz.
$25-37

de KENT Dripless
Penetrating Oil, Windsor Lloyd
Products, Inc., Short, Rect., 4 oz.,
copyright 1937 – **$20-30**

KIBLER'S All 'Round Oil –
"The Universal Oil" Mfg. by
Kibler's All 'Round Oil, Rnd., 4 oz.,
paper label, circa 1930s – **$25-35**

KLEEN-O
Household Machine Oil,
Oval, 4 oz.
$35-45

KLEEN-O
Machine Oil, Gem Products,
Inc., Oval, 4 oz.
$18-25

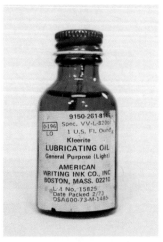

KLEERITE Lubricating
Oil, American Writing Ink
Co., Rnd., 1 oz., brown glass,
circa 1973 – **$10-16**

KLEERITE
Lubricating Oil, American
Writing Ink Co., Inc.,
Rect. 4 oz. – **$10-15**

K & W
Knock'er Loose, Penetrating
Lubricant, Rect., 8 oz.
$8-13

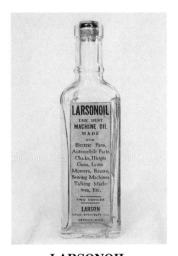

LARSONOIL
The Best Machine Oil,
Larson Drug Specialty Co.,
2 oz. – **$13-19**

LIBERTY OIL CO.
Smoother Oil – The Handy
Household Lubricant,
Oval, 3 oz. – **$27-40**

LIQUID WRENCH
Radiator Specialty Co., Rect.,
16 oz., circa 1943-50s
$15-25

LIQUID WRENCH
Radiator Specialty Co.,
Rect., 8 oz., circa 1943-50s
$13-21

LIQUID WRENCH
Obl., 1 oz.
$15-24

LIQUID WRENCH
Super Lubricating Oil,
Oval, 3 oz., Canada
$25-35

LIQUID WRENCH
Super Rust Solvent
Penetrant, Oval, 3 oz.
$14-24

LIQUID WRENCH
Super Rust Solvent
Penetrant, Oval, 1½ oz.
$11-20

LIQUID WRENCH
The Super Penetrant,
Rect., 8 oz.
$10-18

LIQUID WRENCH
The Super Penetrant,
Oval, 1½ oz.
$11-17

LIQUID WRENCH
Super Lubricant, Rect., 4 oz.
$9-18

LOYD'S
Machine Oil, Oval, 4 oz.
$42-62

LUB-A-SPRAY
All Purpose Dry Lubricant,
Panef Mfg. Co., Inc.,
Rnd., 3 oz. – **$7-12**

LUBRO A High Grade Oil,
J.L. Prescott Co., 1⁵/₈" dia.
x 4¹/₈" tall, paper label,
circa 1920s-30s - **$13-20**

McCORMICK-DEERING
3" dia. x 7¹/₂" tall, scarce
$50+

McNESS
Household Machine Oil,
Furst-McNess Co., 4 oz.
$13-22

MADOL
Household Oil, Rect., 4 oz.
$12-19

MAID OF HONOR
Household Machine Oil,
By Sears, Roebuck & Co.,
Oval, 4 oz. – **$50-70**

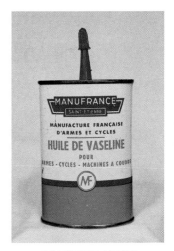

MANUFRANCE
Huile De Vaseline,
Oval, 4 oz., France
$25-35

(The) MANY-USE
Oil, The Many-Use Oil Co.,
1 oz., scarce
$15-25

MARLA
Penetrating Oil,
Rothlan Corp., Oval, 4 oz.,
paper label – **$24-33**

MARVEL
Mystery Oil, Emerol Mfg.
Co., Inc., Obl., 4 oz., price: 30
cents, very scarce – **$30-45**

MARVEL
Mystery Oil, 4 oz.,
with lead spout, scarce
$23-32

MARVEL
Lubricating Oil, Rect., 4 oz.
$12-18

MARVEL
Lubricating Oil, Rnd., 4 oz.,
circa 2000, price: $1.49
$2-4

MASON
Machine Oil, The Perry G.
Mason Co., Rnd., 4 oz.,
scarce – **$35-50**

MASTERCRAFT
Penetrating Oil, Coast to
Coast Stores, Rect., 8 oz.
$9-14

MASTER MECHANIC
Super Oil, Rect., 4 oz.
$5-10

MAYTAG
Household Oil, Rnd., 3 oz.,
(with green wave),
very scarce – **$75+**

MINNEAPOLIS-MOLINE
3" dia. x 7¼" tall
$30-40

MINNEAPOLIS-MOLINE
3" dia. x 7½" tall
$25-35

MITEE
Penetrating Oil, John
Sunshine Chemical Co., Inc.,
Oval, 3 oz. – **$25-35**

MITEE
Penetrating Oil, Dap Inc.,
Obl., 3 oz., circa 1963-73
$13-19

MOR-FILM
Cling Oil, L.R. Kerns Co.,
Rnd., 3 oz., "Complimentary
Sample" – **$20-29**

MR. CHAMP
A Super Penetrating Solvent,
Pyroil Co., Inc., Obl., 3 oz.
$19-29

NEWBRITE
Machine Oil, M.F. Bragdon
Paint Co., Rnd., 16 oz.
$13-17

NOPENCO
All Round Oil, Oval, 3 oz.,
Oslo, Norway
$30-45

NORWESCO Penetrating
Oil, The Northwestern Chemical
Co., Oval, 3 oz., circa 1920s-30s,
extremely scarce – **$65+**

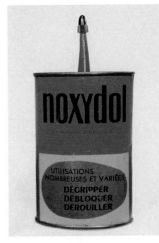

NOXYDOL
Oval, 4 oz., France
$25-35

NYOIL
Mfd. by William F. Nye, 1 oz.,
with box, very scarce
$35-50

O-CEDAR
Machine Oil, O-Cedar of
Canada Ltd., Oval, 4 oz.
$35-50

OCELIUM
Penetrating Oil, Turner
Enterprises, Oval, 3 oz.
$20-30

OILIT
Larkin Co. Inc., Oval, 3 oz.,
circa teens-20s, soldered seams,
extremely scarce – **$95+**

OILIT
Larkin Co. Inc., Oval, 3 oz.,
circa 1920s-30s, very scarce
$65+

OILIT
Larkin Co. Inc.,
Rnd., 2 oz., very scarce
$15-24

O.K.'s OIL
Household Oil, Oval, 4 oz.,
semi-scarce – **$30-40**

OLSON
Instant Release, Oval, 3 oz.
$22-35

General Use Oilers

OPTIMUS
Oval, 4oz., Sweden
$22-33

ORION
Handy Oil, Oval 3 oz.,
Sweden – **$30-40**

OSTER
Super Refined Oil, John
Oster Mfg. Co., Obl., 1 oz.
(dark blue color) – **$14-22**

OSTER
Lubricating Oil, Rnd.,
1/3 oz. – **$8-12**

OUR OWN HARDWARE
3" dia. x 7¼" tall
$25-35

OUR OWN HARDWARE
3" dia. x 7¼" tall
$20-30

OUR OWN HARDWARE
3" dia. x 7¼" tall
$20-30

PANEF
Household Oil, Rnd., 1.6 oz.
$9-17

PANEF
All-Purpose Oil, Rect., 4 oz.
$13-23

PANEF-SMASH
Penetrating Oil & Rust
Solvent, Rect., 4 oz.
$13-23

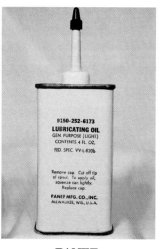

PANEF
Lubricating Oil, Rect., 4 oz.
$13-20

PANEF
Oil, Rnd., 1/2 oz.
$5-7

General Use Oilers

PANEF
Lub-a-Spray Graphite
Lubricant, Rnd., 1/4 oz.
$4-6

PANEF
Lub-a-Lite, Dry White
Lubricant, Rnd., 1/8 oz.
$4-6

PANEF
All-Purpose Oil,
Tall, Rect., 4 oz.
$12-18

PARAMOUNT
Machine Oil, Dist. By Rozelle
Inc., 4 oz., circa 1930s-40s
$14-24

PENETRENE
Austral Chemical Co., Rnd.,
4-5 oz., Australia
$20-30

PENNEX
Pennex Products Co., Inc.,
Oval, 4 oz.
$30-45

PENNEYS
General Use Oil, Rect., 4 oz.,
circa 1960s
$25-35

PERFECT
White Oil, Rect., 4 oz.,
Belgium
$20-30

PERFECTION
Machine Oil,
Avon Products, Inc., 3 oz.
$18-28

PERMATEX
Solvo-Rust, Super Penetrant,
Rect., 16 oz., "Sample Can"
$10-18

PERMATEX
Solvo-Rust, Rect., 8 oz.
$12-20

PERMATEX
Solvo-Rust, Super Penetrant,
Rect., 3 oz.
$16-25

GENERAL USE OILERS

PETRINGS
Trumpet Brand Machine Oil,
H.P. Coffee Co., 4 oz.
$15-25

PETROLEUM
2³/₈" wd. x ⁷/₈"dp. x 7³/₈" tall,
soldered seams; leather
washers, Germany – **$25-35**

PREMIUM
Household Oil, Rect., 4 oz.
$25-34

PREMIUM
Quality Household Oil,
Rect., 8 oz.
$7-14

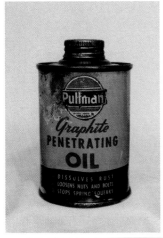

PULLMAN
Graphite Penetrating Oil,
Universal Chemical Co.,
Rnd., 8 oz. – **$20-27**

PURITAN
Penetrant, Olin Mathieson
Chemical Corp., Rect., 8 oz.
$20-30

PYROIL All Purpose Lubricant, 12-pc. Store counter display,
3 oz. cans - 25 cents each, pat.
1932, extremely scarce – **$300+**

PYROIL
All Purpose Lubricant, 3 oz.,
Household Size
$15-25

PYROIL
Penetrating Oil (P),
Rect., 8 oz.
$10-18

RADIANT No. 857 Lubricating
Oil, Midway Chemical Co., Tall,
Rect., 12 oz., circa 1930s,
very scarce – **$70-90**

RADIANT
Machine Oil, Midway
Chemical Co., 4 oz.
$19-29

RADIANT
Household Machine Oil,
Midway Chemical Co., 4 oz.
$16-26

41

RADIANT
Machine Oil, Boyle-Midway
Inc., Oval, 4 oz.,
circa 1940s-50s – **$15-25**

RADIANT
Machine Oil, Rect., 4 oz.
$22-32

RADIANT
Household Oil, Tall, Obl., 4
oz., price: 29 cents
$19-28

RAWLEIGH'S Ideal Oil,
The W.T. Rawleigh Co.,
Rect., 8 oz.
$12-21

RAYCINE
Super Refined Oil, Obl., 1
oz., (black color)
$14-23

RED DIAMOND
Household Machine Oil,
Rect., 4 oz.
$30-45

RELEASEALL
Penetrating Oil, Oval, 4 oz.,
paper label, Canada
$22-32

RELEASEALL
Rust Solvent & Penetrant,
Oval, 4 oz., Canada,
"Replicated" – **$22-32**

RENAULT
Huile Vaseline,
Oval, 4 oz., France
$25-35

REVELATION
General Use Oil, Oval, 4 oz.,
Canada – **$20-30**

RITE-WAY
Machine Oil, Oval, 4 oz.
$45-60

RITE-WAY
Machine Oil, Cardinal
Laboratories, Inc., Oval, 4 oz.
$38-50

RIVERSIDE
Penetrating Oil, Montgomery
Ward, Rect., 8 oz.
$12-20

RONSON Oily Bird,
Household Lubricant, Rect.,
5 oz., price: 1 pound – 6
pence, England – **$26-37**

ROYAL
General Purpose Oil,
Tall, Obl., 4 oz.
$22-30

RUST-OFF
Penetrating Oil, The Capo
Polishes Ltd., Oval, 4 oz.,
Canada – **$17-25**

RUST RUNNER
Penetrating Oil, Rect., 8 oz.,
paper label – **$10-17**

SARGENT
Household Machine Oil,
Sargent Mfg. Co., Rect., 4 oz.
$23-31

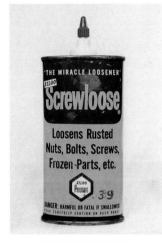

SCREWLOOSE
"The Miracle Loosener",
Oval, 4 oz., price: 39 cents
$13-19

SEARS
Super Penetrating Oil, Oval,
4 oz., paper label, Canada
$16-26

SEARS
Graphite Penetrating Oil,
Rect., 4 oz.
$17-24

SEARS
Penetrating Oil, Rect., 4 oz.
$18-24

SHAPLEIGH HARDWARE
Norleigh Diamond Oiler,
3" dia. x 7" tall, semi-scarce
$30-40

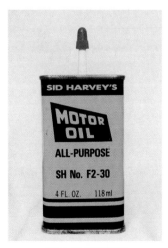

SID HARVEY
All Purpose Motor Oil,
Rect., 4 oz.
$13-21

SIGNET OIL
Russia Cement Co., 1 oz.,
price: 10 cents, very scarce
$35-45

SIGNET OIL
Russia Cement Co.,
Oval, 1 oz.
$35-45

SIGNPOST
Lubricating Oil, Wide, Oval,
7½ oz., England, very scarce
(front view) – **$75+**

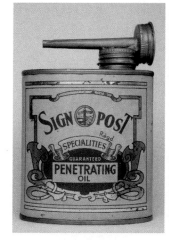

SIGNPOST
(back view)

SIMONS Penetrating Graphite
Oil, The Simonize Co., 2" dia. x
5¼" tall reservoir with 5" spout,
circa 1930s, very scarce – **$55-75**

SINGER
Household Oil,
Oval, 3 oz., semi-scarce
$26-35

SINGER
Household Oil,
Oval, 1⅓ oz., semi-scarce
$24-33

SLADE'S
Machine Oil, Guaranteed by
Chas. F. Slade Co., Inc.,
2 oz. with box – **$17-25**

SLIPCO
General Purpose Oil, Wide
Oval, 7½ oz., Great Britian
$27-36

SNOW BIRD
Machine Oil, Oval, 4 oz.,
circa 1930s, very scarce
$90+

SNOW BIRD
Machine Oil, Oval, 3 oz.,
circa 1930s-40s, very scarce
$80+

SNOW BIRD
Machine Oil, Oval, 4 oz.,
circa 1940s, very scarce
$65+

SNOW BIRD
Machine Oil,
6 oz., circa 1940s
$16-24

SNOW BIRD
Machine Oil, 6 oz.,
circa 1940s-50s
$14-22

SOUTHERN HOME
Machine Oil, Garlinger &
Co., Inc., 4 oz.
$13-21

STOWE SUPPLY CO.
2³/4" dia. x 7¹/4" tall, scarce
$60-80

STURMEY ARCHER
Oil, Sturmey-Archer Gears
Ltd., Rect., 8 oz., England
$17-27

SUPERFINE
Handy Oil, Oval, 3 oz.
$23-30

SUPREME
General Use Oil, Supreme
Chemical Co., Rect., 4 oz.
$18-28

SURE SHOT
Handy Oil, National Drugs
Inc., Oval, 3 oz.
$30-40

TENK HARDWARE CO.
2³/4" dia. x 8" tall,
circa Turn of the Century
$35-45

TERMOX
Machine Oil, Termox
Chemical Co., 3 oz.
$13-20

**THREE-IN-ONE/G.W.
COLE CO.,** (George W. Cole
founder of 3-in-1 oil) 3oz., no label,
circa about 1895, very scarce – **$25-30**

**THREE-IN-ONE/
G.W. COLE CO.,**
1 oz. – no label, circa about
1895, very scarce – **$20-25**

THREE-IN-ONE
"Sample" octagonal, 3/4" wd. x
2 3/8" tall, circa pre-1910,
very scarce – **$18-25**

3-IN-ONE
Oiler, 2 1/8" dia. x 3"tall, "Refill only with 3-in-One...all
dealers...two size bottles" circa about 1895-1905, (oldest 3-
in-One oiler seen thus far) extremely scarce – **$70+**

3-IN-ONE "Free Sample", 1/2"
dia. x 1 3/4" tall, paper label
floats inside, Pat. Nov. 18,
1902, very scarce – **$13-20**

THREE-IN-ONE OIL CO.
Wood Mailing box for 1 oz. bottle, 5" wd. x
2 5/8" dp. x 1 5/8" tall, extremely scarce
(without bottle) – **$20-35**

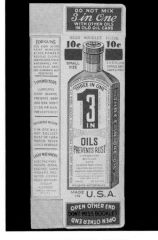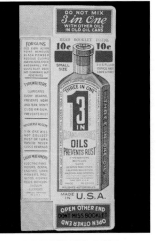

THREE-IN-ONE
Unused box for 1 oz. bottle
$10-15

3-IN-ONE OILS
Oilright Handy Can, Oval,
1oz., price 15 cents, circa
1922+, scarce – **$28-39**

3-IN-ONE-OIL
"Sample" – "Cleans, Oils,
Protects", triangular 1 7/8" long,
(clear glass), scarce – **$15-20**

3-IN-ONE-OIL
"Free Sample", 1/2" dia. x 1 3/4"
tall, paper label floats inside,
scarce – **$10-17**

3-IN-ONE-OIL
Oval, 3 oz., (front & back
mirror each other),
semi-scarce – **$38-50**

3-IN-ONE OIL
Oval, 1 oz.
$30-38

THREE IN ONE OILS
1 oz., (green glass)
$15-22

THREE IN ONE OILS
1 oz. with box, Canada
$32-40

3-IN-ONE OIL
The A.S. Boyle Co., 1 oz.,
(green glass)
$18-23

3-IN-ONE OIL
Oval, 1 oz., scarce
$29-36

3-IN-ONE OIL
Oval, 3 oz., (Good
Housekeeping seal on side)
$27-36

3-IN-ONE OIL
Obl., 3 oz.
$13-23

3-IN-ONE OIL
Heavy Body Oil, Obl. 3 oz.
$15-25

3-IN-ONE OIL
Heavy Body Oil, Obl., 1 oz.
$15-25

3-IN-ONE OIL
Boyle-Midway Inc.,
Rect. 3 oz., unusual size
$22-32

3-IN-ONE OIL
Obl., 1 oz.
$13-20

3-IN-ONE OIL
Heavy Body Oil, Obl., 3 oz.,
(Good Housekeeping
seal on side) – **$12-18**

3-IN-ONE OIL
Heavy Body Oil, Obl., 1 oz.
(Good Housekeeping
seal on side) – **$12-18**

3-IN-ONE
Electric Motor Oil, Obl., 3 oz.
$12-16

3-IN-ONE OIL
Obl., 1 oz., (silver color)
$9-13

3-IN-ONE
Electric Motor Oil, "Bellows
Oiler", Rect., 8 oz.
$14-24

3-IN-ONE OIL
Boyle-Midway Inc., Rect.,
8 oz., "Economy Size"
$14-24

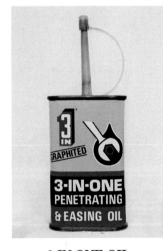

3-IN-ONE OIL
Penetrating & Easing Oil,
Rect., 3.5 oz., England
(front view) – **$25-35**

3-IN-ONE
Penetrating & Easing Oil
(Back View)

3-IN-ONE
Electric Motor Oil, Obl., 3 oz.,
(silver color)
$9-14

3-IN-ONE OIL
Obl., 1 oz., (silver color)
$8-11

3-IN-ONE
Electric Motor Oil,
Obl., 3 oz., Canada
$9-12

3-IN-ONE
Bolt Loosener, Rect.,
8 oz., Canada
$9-17

3-IN-ONE
Bolt Loosener, Obl., 3 oz.
$5-10

3-IN-ONE
Multi-Purpose Oil, Obl., 3 oz.
$2-5

TOM THUMB
Graphite Penetrating Oil,
Rnd., 4.26 oz., circa 1968
$14-22

TOTAL
Oval 5 oz., France
$20-30

TRANSYL
1½" dia. x 3½" tall,
Dutch, paper label, scarce
$25-35

TRIPLE-X
Electric Motor Oil, Triple-X
Chemical Laboratories, Rect.,
8 oz. – **$10-17**

TRU-TEST
Household Oil, "War
Package", Rnd., 4 oz.,
paper label – **$12-18**

TRUE VALUE
Household Oil, Hibbard,
Spencer, Bartlett & Co.,
Oval, 4 oz. – **$40-65**

TRUE VALUE
Lubricating Oil, Hibbard,
Spencer, Bartlett & Co.,
Oval, 4 oz. – **$40-60**

TUMBLER
Penetrating Oil, Rect., 8 oz.
$10-28

UNICO
Household Oil, Packaged for
United Co-Operatives, Inc.,
Rect., 4 oz. – **$24-32**

**UNITED TECHNICAL
LUBRICANTS** Household
Oil, United Petroleum Corp.,
Oval, 4 oz. – **$35-45**

U-OIL
Oilwell Oiler, Oval, 1 oz.,
Canada, "Replicated", scarce
$25-35

VAN CAMP OIL
Van Camp Hardware and
Iron Co., Oval, 3 oz., circa
1930s, very scarce – **$50-70**

VANTROL
Anti-Rust Precision Oil, Van
Straaten Chemical Co.,
Oval, 3 oz. – **$23-33**

VANTROL
Anti-Rust Precision Oil,
Oval, 3 oz.
$19-29

VARCON (by Gambles)
Graphited Penetrating
Lubricant, Obl., 3 oz.
$15-24

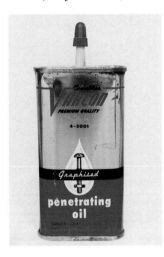

VARCON
(by Gambles), Graphited
Penetrating Oil, Obl., 3 oz.
$20-30

VARCON
(by Gambles), Light Machine
& General Purpose Oil,
Obl., 3 oz. – **$18-28**

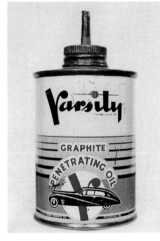

VARSITY Graphite
Penetrating Oil, Varsity
Products Co., Rnd., 8 oz.,
Copyright 1937 – **$28-36**

VARSITY
Graphite Penetrating Oil,
Rect., 8 oz.
$17-27

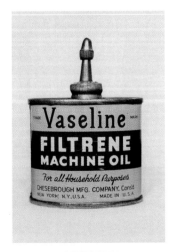

VASELINE
Filtrene Machine Oil,
Chesebrough Mfg. Co., Oval,
1½oz., very scarce – **$40-60**

VEECO
Household Oil, The American
Products Co., Oval, 4 oz.
$30-40

VEECO
Household Oil, "War Time
Package", 4 oz. – **$26-33**

VEECO
Household Oil, 4 oz.
$23-30

General Use Oilers

VELOX
Super Huile De Vaseline,
Rect., 125 ml., France
$17-27

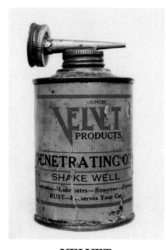

VELVET
Velvet Specialty Co., Rnd.,
8 oz., paper label, circa
1930s-40s – **$17-27**

VISCO
Penetrating Oil, The Visco
Chemical Products Co., Oval,
3 oz., scarce – **$40-60**

WAKEFIELD Everyman's
Oil, C.C. Wakefield & Co.,
Ltd., wide oval, 7 1/2 oz.,
England, scarce – **$50-70**

WAKEFIELD
Everyman's Oil, wide oval,
7 1/2 oz., England, scarce
$45-60

WALLER
Household Oil, M. Waller
Corp., Oval, 4 oz., circa
1930s-40s – **$28-35**

WARCO
Penetrant, Warwick
Laboratories, Oval, 4 oz.
$30-40

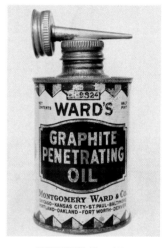

WARD'S Graphite
Penetrating Oil, Montgomery
Ward & Co., Rnd., 8 oz., circa
1930s-40s – **$20-30**

WARDS
Fine Machine Oil, Oval, 4 oz.
$35-50

WARDS
Fine Machine Oil, Oval, 4 oz.
$30-40

WARNER
Penetreen, Warner-Patterson
Co., Rnd., 4 oz.,
circa 1930s-40s – **$24-33**

WATKINS
Machine Oil, The J.R.
Watkins Co., Oval, 3 oz.,
scarce – **$28-38**

WATKINS
Machine Oil, Rnd., 8 oz.
$16-24

WAY-MAT OIL
Wayne Materials Corp.,
Rnd., 1 oz.
$6-10

WESTERN'S SUPREME
Fine Parts Oil, Western Auto
Supply Co., Rect., 4 oz.
$25-35

WHIZ No. 4 Oil, The R.M. Hollingshead Co., "...touch each bearing w/
broom straw dipped in oil" 3oz., circa
1910-20s, extremely scarce – **$125+**

WHIZ OIL
For General Use, Oval, 4 oz.,
circa 1920s-early 30s,
very scarce – **$200+**

WHIZ
General Use Oil, Oval,
4 oz., scarce
$55-75

WHIZ
Mechanics Loosen-All,
Rect., 4 oz., circa 1950s
$20-28

WHIZ
Hollingshead,
General Use Oil, Rect., 4oz.
$17-27

WHIZ
Super Loosen-All, Rect., 8 oz.
$13-18

**WICHITA MUNICIPAL
FEDERAL CREDIT UNION**
Rnd., 1/3 oz.,
(label floats in oil) – **$5-10**

WILCO
Machine Oil, 4 oz.,
with lead spout
$25-35

WILCO
Machine Oil, Obl., 3 oz.
$25-35

WILCO
Home & Shop Machine Oil,
Obl., 3oz.
$22-32

WITTROCK'S XLNT
Household Lubricating Oil,
L.R. Wittrock Mfg., Co., 4 oz.
$13-23

WIZARD
Dripless Oil, Western Auto
Supply Co., short Rect., 4 oz.
$20-28

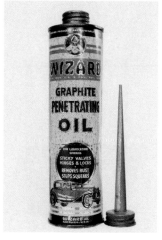

WIZARD
Graphite Penetrating Oil,
Wizard Inc., Rnd., 10 oz., circa
1930s, very scarce – **$50-65**

WIZARD
Machine Oil, Wizard Inc.,
Oval, 3oz., copyright 1933,
very scarce – **$85+**

WIZARD
Honor-Brite Machine Oil,
Wizard, Inc., Oval, 3 oz.,
scarce, "replicated" – **$40-60**

WRENCHO
Serco Products, Oval, 3 oz.
$27-37

WYNN'S
Utility Oil, Obl., 3 oz.
$17-25

Z-4
Penetrating All-In-One Oil,
Rect., 4 oz.
$15-25

ZACO
Penetrating Oil, The Zip
Abrasive Co., Oval, 3 oz.,
circa 1920s-30s, scarce – **$29-38**

ZENITH
Household Oil, Marshall-Wells
Co., Rnd., 4 oz.,
with 3" spout, scarce – **$28-36**

ABERCROMBIE & FITCH CO.
Gun Oil, Oval, 3 oz., paper label, very scarce – **$85+**

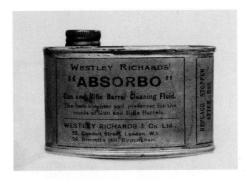

ABSORBO
Gun & Rifle Barrel Cleaning Fluid, Westley Richards' & Co., Ltd., Oval, 3 1/8" wd. x 1 1/2" dp. x 2 1/8" tall, paper label, England, extremely scarce
$100+

ABU GARCIA OIL
1/4 oz. tube
$3-8

ALCAN
Fine Gun Oil, Rnd. 1/2 oz.
$10-20

ALOX
Lubricating Oil, Alox Corp., Oval, 4 oz.
$19-27

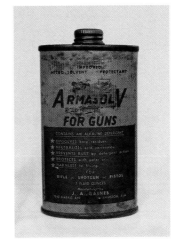

ARMASOLV
For Guns, J.A. Gaines, Oval, 3 oz., paper label
$35-48

BARDAHL
Sportsmen's Oil, Oval, 3 oz.
$40-60

BILL'S 13
Real Reel Oil, Dean Brothers, 1/2 oz.
$10-20

BIRCHWOOD CASEY
Bore Solvent, Rect., 4 oz., circa 1963-73
$10-17

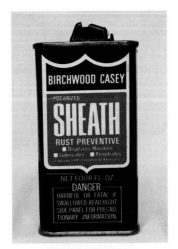

BIRCHWOOD CASEY
Sheath Rust Preventive, Rect., 4 oz., circa 1963-73
$11-18

BRITE-BORE
Gun Oil, Mill-Rose Co., short Rect., 4 oz.
$40-60

BRITE-BORE
Nitro Powder Solvent, Mill
Run Products Co., Rect., 4 oz.
$19-28

BRITE-BORE
Gun Oil, Mill Run Products
Co., Rect., 4 oz.
$19-28

BRITE-BORE
Lubricating Oil, 2 oz.
$4-8

BRONSON
Reel Oil, Bronson Reel Co.,
1" sq. x 2¾" tall
$14-24

BROWNING
Honing Oil, Rect., 4 oz.
$23-40

BROWNING OIL
Rect., 4 oz.
$23-33

B.S.A. "KLEENWELL" OIL
B.S.A. Guns Ltd., Oval, 3 oz.,
England, very scarce
$100+

B.S.A.
Scientific Cleaners, 4-piece kit,
(open view)

B.S.A. SCIENTIFIC CLEANERS
For Guns & Rifles, 4-piece kit, England,
very scarce, (closed view)
$260+

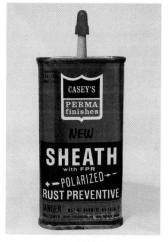

CASEY'S
New Sheath Rust
Preventive, Obl., 3 oz.
$11-19

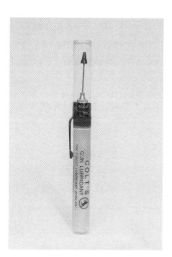

COLT'S
Gun Lubricant,
Rnd., ¼ oz., tube
$12-20

COMPLETE
Gun Care, Dri-Power Co.,
Oval, 3 oz., (front view)
$50-75

COMPLETE
Gun Care, (back view)

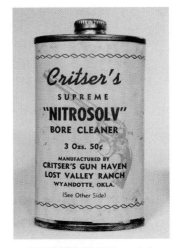

CRITSER'S "Nitrosolv"
Bore Cleaner, Critser's Gun
Haven, Lost Valley Ranch, Oval,
3 oz., paper label, scarce – **$50-70**

DAISY Gun Oil,
Gun Oil for BB Guns,
Sq. 1/2 oz.
$9-15

DAISY
Touch-Up (Gun-Blu)
Sq. 1/2 oz.
$9-15

DAISY
Sportsman's Penetrating Oil
& Rust Solvent, Rnd., 1.6 oz.
$17-27

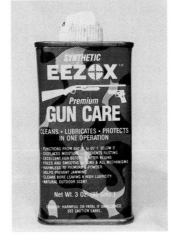

EEZOX
Premium Gun Care,
Rect., 3 oz.
$14-24

FIENDOIL
"Sample",
3/4" dia. x 17/8" tall, scarce
$37-49

FIENDOIL
"Sample" – 7/8" dia. x 21/4"
tall, scarce
$34-45

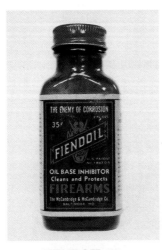

FIENDOIL The
McCambridge & McCambridge
Co., 2 oz. (brown glass), price 35
cents, pat. 1932 – **$29-40**

FIENDOIL
Rust Preventive Lubricant,
Sq. 1/4 oz.
$20-30

FULCRUM
Gun & Reel Oil, 1/2 oz.
$12-19

Gun/Military/Reel/Sportsmans Oilers

FULCRUM
Gun & Reel Oil, 1 oz.
$23-30

GUN-GUARDIAN Rust
Preventive Oil, Guardian Vapor
Products Co., Rect., 4 oz., paper
label, circa 1963-73 – **$25-35**

GUNSLICK
Lawn Mower Oil, Mfd. by Outers
Laboratories, Rect., 5 oz., very
scarce (front view) – **$50-70**

GUNSLICK
Lawn Mower Oil
(back view)

GUNSLICK
Gun Oil, Outers
Laboratories, Rect., 1 oz.,
(blue glass) – **$20-30**

H-R SOLVENT
Harrington Richardson Arms
Co., Oval, 3 oz., paper label,
extremely scarce – **$95+**

HERTER'S Silicone
Lubricant for Reels & Guns,
1/2 oz. – copyright 1953, price
75 cents/3 shillings – **$10-19**

HERTER'S
Dry Fly Oil, Sq. 1 oz.
$16-24

J.C. HIGGINS
Reel Oil, Sears,
Roebuck & Co., 1 oz.
$13-20

J.C. HIGGINS
Reel Oil, 1 oz.
$10-18

HOPPE'S Nitro Powder
Solvent, Frank A. Hoppe,
Inc., Rnd., 3 oz.,
large lettering & #9 – **$20-30**

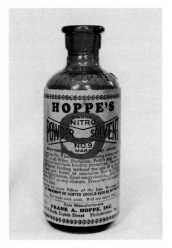

HOPPE'S
Nitro Powder Solvent,
Rnd., 3 oz.
$16-26

57

Gun/Military/Reel/Sportsmans Oilers

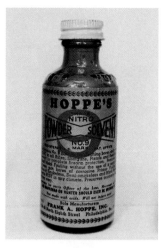

HOPPE'S
Nitro Powder Solvent,
Rnd., 3 oz.
$10-20

ITHACA
Gun Oil, Ithaca Gun Co.,
Oval, 4 oz., extremely scarce
$300+

JENOLITE
Gun Oil, Rect., 120 ml,
France, "Replicated"
$20-30

MARBLE'S
Nitro-Solvent Oil, Marble
Safety Axe Co., 2 oz., price 25
cents, very scarce – **$100+**

MARLIN
Special Gun Oil, Marlin
Firearms Co., 2 oz., scarce
$30-45

MASTERCRAFT
Gun Oil, Coast to Coast
Stores, Oval, 3 oz.
$40-50

MASTERCRAFT
Gun Oil, Oval, 3 oz.
$30-45

OLD HI'S
Reel & Utility Oil, Horrocks-
Ibbotson Co., Obl., 1 oz.
$18-28

OUTERS
Gun Oil, Oval, 3 oz.
$19-30

OUTERS
Gun Oil, Obl., 3 oz.
$13-18

OUTERS
Gun Oil, Obl., 3 oz., paper
label over painted can
$30-45

PACIFIC Klean Kwick Gun
Oil, Pacific Gun Sight Co.,
Oval, 3½ oz., paper label, circa
1920s-30s, very scarce –**$150+**

58

PALMA COMPOUND
Palma Products Co.,
Oval, 3 oz.
$28-38

PELL GUN OIL
Crossman-Hahn,
Rnd., 1/8 oz.
$9-16

PFLUEGER
Dryfly Oil – No. 879, 1/2 oz.
$8-14

PFLUEGER
Speede Oil, 1 oz.
$4-7

PFLUEGER
Speede Reel Oil,
1 oz., paper label
$4-7

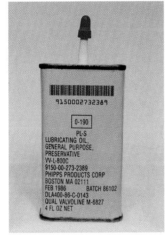

PHIPPS Products Corp.,
PL-S Lubricating Oil,
Rect., 4 oz., circa 1986
$10-15

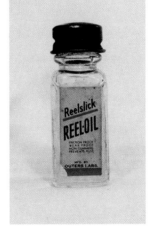

REELSLICK
Reel-Oil, By Outers Labs.,
7/8" sq. x 2 1/4" tall
$12-19

REELSLICK
Reel-Oil, 1/2 oz.
$8-12

REELSLICK
Dry Fly Oil, 1/2 oz.
$9-15

REMINGTON
Rem Oil, 3/4" dia. x 3 3/8" tall
with box , very scarce
$40-50

REMINGTON
Powder Solvent, Remington
Arms Co., Inc., Oval, 3 oz.,
scarce – **$60-80**

REM OIL
Oval, 3 oz.
$50-70

SAVAGE Gun Oil,
Savage Arms Corp.,
Oval, 3 oz.
$85+

SAVAGE
Solvent, Rnd., 2 oz.
$30-40

SCHRADE
Honing Oil, Rect.,
4 oz., paper label
$25-35

SEAL-S-TEEL X-Ring
Products Co., Oval, 3 oz.,
paper label, circa 1920s-30s,
extremely scarce – **$150+**

SEARS
Nitro Powder Solvent, 2 oz.
$17-27

SEARS
Gun Oil, "Ted Williams",
Oval, 3 oz., paper label
$48-65

SEARS
Reel Oil, 1 oz.
$10-15

SEARS
Gun Oil, "Ted Williams",
Oval, 3 oz., paper label,
circa 1963-73 – **$40-60**

SEARS
Gun Oil, "Ted Williams" Obl.,
3 oz., circa 1963-73
$30-48

SHAKESPEARE
Perfect Reel Oil, 1/2 oz.,
brown glass
$20-28

SHAKESPEARE
One Drop Reel Oil,
1/2 oz., brown glass
$16-25

SHEATH
Rust Preventive for Sports,
Rnd., 3 oz., (front left view)
$17-27

SHEATH
(front right view)

SHEATH
Rust Preventive
for Sports, 3 oz.
$12-24

SHRADER'S Wonder Penetrating & Rust Dissolving Oil, G.W. Shrader -Gunsmith, Oval, 3 oz., circa 1920s-30s, extremely scarce – **$150+**

SHURE KLEEN
W.E. Binko, Oval, 3 oz., pat. 1937, price 35 cents, scarce
$80+

SOUTH BEND
Precision Oiler, Rnd., 1/4 oz.
$11-22

STAG
Gun Oil, Oval, 3 oz.
$30-40

STAG
Gun Oil, Oval, 3 oz.
$20-32

STOEGEROL The Combination Gun Oil & Solvent, A.F. Stoeger, Inc., Oval, 3 oz., price 50 cents, extremely scarce – **$250+**

STOEGEROL The Combination Gun Oil & Solvent, Stoeger Arms Corp., Oval, 3 oz., price 50 cents, extremely scarce – **$270+**

STOEGEROL The Combination Oil, "...and is a wound sterilizer", A.F. Stoeger, Oval, 3 oz., price $1, extremely scarce – **$225**

STOEGER
London Oil Finish, Stoeger Arms Corp., Rnd., 4 oz., semi-scarce – **$50-80**

STOEGEROL
Gun Oil, Stoeger Arms Corp., Rnd., 4 oz., semi-scarce
$50-80

Gun/Military/Reel/Sportsmans Oilers

STOEGER
Gunsmith Bluer, Stoeger
Arms Corp., 2" sq. x 2³/4" tall
glass bottle, scarce – **$30-45**

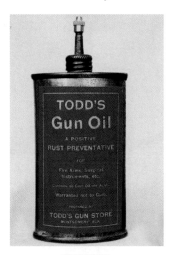

TODD'S
Gun Oil, Todd's Gun Store,
Oval, 3 oz., paper label, circa
1920s-30s, very scarce –**$45-60**

TRULINE
Gun Oil, Eaton's of Canada,
Rect., 4 oz., paper label, circa
1950s – **$70+**

TRULINE
Gun Solvent, Eaton's of
Canada, Rect., 4 oz., paper
label, circa 1950s –**$70+**

TWO-WAY
Lubrication Kit (oil & grease)
Wright & McGill, Rnd., 1.6 cc
grease/5.4 cc oil – **$7-12**

VANTROL
Gun & Reel Oil, Van
Straaten Chemical Co., Oval,
3 oz., circa 1943-50s – **$65-85**

WARDS
Reel Oil,
Montgomery Ward, 1/2 oz.
$9-18

WARDS
Western Field Gun Oil,
2 oz., brown glass
$22-29

WARDS
Western Field, Nitro Powder
Solvent, 2 oz.
$22-27

WARDS
Hawthorne, Nitro Powder
Solvent, 2 oz.
$23-30

WARDS Western Field
Gun Cleaning Solvent,
Rnd., 2 oz., brown glass
$12-22

(Montgomery) WARD
Gun Oil, Obl., 3 oz.,
circa 1963-73
$12-20

WEBLEY Oil
Webley & Scott Ltd., Oval,
4 oz., England/New Zealand,
very scarce – **$100+**

WILCO
Gun Oil, Obl., 3 oz.
$35-50

WILLIAMS
Bore Cleaner,
Williams Gun Sight Co., Oval,
3 oz., price 60 cents – **$30-45**

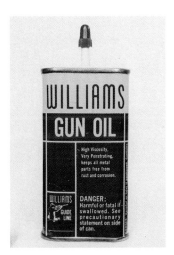

WILLIAMS
Gun Oil, Obl., 3 oz.
$30-45

WYNOIL
Special Firearm Oil, Oval,
4 oz., paper label, price 35
cents, scarce – **$85+**

DIXON Lock-Ease
Lock Fluid, The Joseph
Dixon Crucible Co., Short
Rect., 4 oz. – **$19-29**

DIXON
Lock-Ease Lock Fluid,
Short Rect., 4 oz.
$16-25

DIXON
Lock Mate, Rect., 4 oz.
$12-18

INGERSOLL Lok-Eeze
(powdered graphite) 4¼" tall,
plastic figure of English Police-
man, England, scarce – **$35-50**

KLEEN-FLO
Lock De-Icer, Oval, 4 oz.
$20-29

LOCK-EASE (AGS)
American Grease Stick Co.,
3.4 oz, plastic
$8-12

PANEF
Lub-a-Lock
Lock Lubricant, Rect., 4 oz.
$13-18

TWENTIETH CENTURY
Dripless Penetrating Oil,
Short Rect., 4 oz.
$19-28

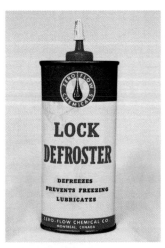

ZERO-FLOW Chemicals,
Lock Defroster, Zero-Flow
Chemical Co., Oval, 4 oz.,
Canada – **$25-37**

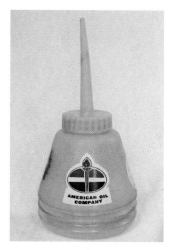

AMERICAN OIL COMPANY
3³/8" dia. x 6³/4" tall
$20-29

AMOCO
Home Oil, The American Oil
Co., Oval, 4 oz., circa 1930,
extremely scarce – **$150+**

AMOCO
Home Oil, (advertisement)
circa 1930

AMOCO
Home Oil, Rnd., 4 oz.
$18-29

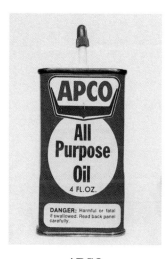

APCO
All Purpose Oil, Rect., 4 oz.
$23-29

A-PENN
All-Purpose
Machine Oil, 3 oz.
$17-25

A-PENN
All-Purpose Machine Oil,
3 oz., price 10 cents
$12-18

ARCHER
Utility Oil, ¹/2 oz.
$5-10

ATLAS Penetrating Six In One
Oil, Penn City Oil Corp., Rect.,
4 oz., circa 1930s, extremely
scarce (front view) – **$120**

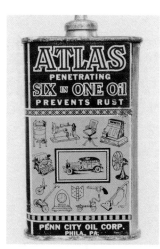

ATLAS
(back view)

B/A Household Oil,
The British American Oil
Co., Oval, 4 oz., circa late
1960s, Canada – **$50-60**

B/A
Handy Oiler, Rnd.,
¹/2 oz., Canada
$9-13

BLUE VELVET
Handy Oiler, Kerr-McGee
Refining Corp., Rnd., 1/2oz.
circa 1963-73 – **$9-16**

BORON
Home Oiler, Rect., 4 oz.
$25-35

BORON
Penetrating Oil, Rect., 4 oz.
$18-25

BP
Energol – Domestic Oil,
Rect., 4 oz., Sweden, scarce
$60-75

BP
Energol – Domestic Oil,
Rect., 4 oz., United Kingdom
$50-65

BP
Home Lubricating Oil,
Rect., 4 oz., Canada
$27-37

BP
Household Oil, Rect., 4 oz.
$40-50

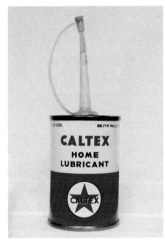

CALTEX
Home Lubricant, Rnd., 3 oz,
Australia, scarce
$60-75

CALTEX
Domestic Lubricant, Rect.,
4 oz., France, scarce
$50-60

CALTEX
Home Lubricant, Rect.,
4 oz., Australia
$60-70

CALTEX
Home Lubricant, Rect.,
4 oz., Australia
$30-40

CALTEX
Home Lubrication Kit,
31/2 oz. tubes, Australia
$22-30

Oil Company Oilers

CANADIAN TIRE CORP.
Heavy Body Machine Oil
Oval, 4 oz., Canada
$25-35

CANADIAN TIRE CORP.
Extra-Fine Machine Oil,
Oval, 4 oz., Canada
$25-35

CANADIAN TIRE CORP.
Heavy-Body Machine Oil,
Oval, 4 oz., Canada
$25-35

CANADIAN TIRE CORP.
Rnd. 1/3 oz., Canada
$8-12

CASTROL
Everyman Oil, Rect. 4 oz.,
England – **$30-50**

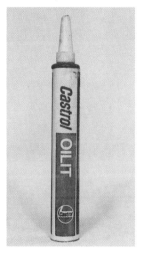

CASTROL Oilit
Rnd., 1/2 oz.
$10-14

CASTROL Oilit
A Good All Purpose Oil,
Rnd., 1/2 oz.
$8-12

CHEVRON
RPM Handy Oil, Rect., 4 oz.
$20-27

CITGO
Utility Oil, Rect., 4 oz.
$15-21

CITIES SERVICE
Penetrating Oil, Rect., 4 oz.,
Pat. 1926, extremely scarce
$100+

CITIES SERVICE OILS
Penetrating Oil, Rnd., 8 oz.,
very scarce – **$28-45**

CITIES SERVICE OILS
Penetrating Oil, Rnd., 3 oz.,
circa 1920s-30s, very scarce
$95+

67

— Oil Company Oilers —

CITIES SERVICE
Utility Oil, Rnd., 4 oz.,
painted label
$25-35

CITIES SERVICE
Penetrating Oil, Rnd., 8 oz.
$15-25

CITIES SERVICE
Utility Oil, 4 oz.
$35-50

CITIES SERVICE
Penetrating Oil, Rect., 8 oz.
$25-35

CITIES SERVICE
Penetrating Oil, Oval, 4 oz.
$30-40

CITIES SERVICE
Utility Oil, 3/4 oz., plastic,
semi-scarce
$28-39

CITIES SERVICE
Penetrating Oil, Rect., 4 oz.
$14-19

CONOCO
Continental Oil Co., Rnd.,
4 oz., extremely scarce
(front view) – **$300+**

CONOCO
(side view)

CONOCO
Germ Processed Anti-Squeak
Oil, Oval, 3 oz., semi-scarce
$33-52

CONOCO Germ Processed
Light Machine Oil, Oval, 3
oz., semi-scarce, (front view)
$33-52

CONOCO
(back view)

CONOCO
Household Oil, Rect., 4 oz.
$14-25

CO-OP
Household Oil, Oval,
4 oz., scarce
$65-80

CO-OP
Household Oil, Obl., 3 oz.
$22-31

CO-OP
Household Oil,
Rect., 4 oz.
$12-18

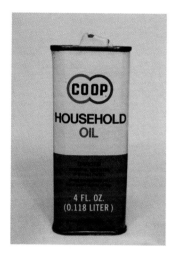

CO-OP
Household Oil,
Tall, obl., 4 oz.
$12-18

DIAMOND Household Oil,
Mid-Continent Petroleum
Corp., Rect., 4 oz., very
scarce – **$50-70**

EL PASO
General Use Oil, El Paso
National Gas Prod. Co.,
Rect., 4 oz. – **$30-45**

EN-AR-CO Canadian Oil
Companies Ltd., 1⅝" dia. x
4¼" tall reservoir with 4"-6"
spout, very scarce – **$45-65**

EN-AR-CO The National
Refining Co., Oval, 3 oz.,
circa 1930s, extremely scarce
(front view) – **$300+**

EN-AR-CO
(back view)

ENCO
Rust-Ban 392, Rect., 4 oz.
$15-24

ESSO
Handy Oil, Rect. 4 oz.,
circa late 1930s, Canada,
scarce – **$50-68**

ESSOLUBE Anglo-American Oil Co., Ltd. 2¾" wd. x 1⅜" dp. x 4¼" tall. Believed to be salesman's sample of 1-gal. can. England, very scarce – **$70-90**

ESSO
Aviation Instrument Oil, Oval, 3 oz., very scarce
$100+

ESSO
Handy Oil, Esso Incorporated, Oval, 3 oz.
$30-40

ESSO
Handy Oil, Atlantic Union Oil Co., Ltd., Oval, 4 oz., Australia – **$70-90**

ESSO
Handy Oil, Obl., 3 oz. (red, white & blue colors)
$50+

ESSO
Handy Oil, Obl., 1 oz., (red, white, & blue colors)
$30-43

ESSO Handy Oil, Esso of Canada Ltd. – A Div. of Imperial Oil Ltd., Rect., 4 oz., (red, white & black colors) – **$50-65**

ESSO
Oval, 90 cm, Finland, scarce
$30-50

ESSO
Handy Oil, Oval, 90 cc, Holland, scarce
$60-75

ESSO
Handy Oil, Rect., 4 oz., Australia – **$50-70**

ESSO
Handy Oil, Rect., 4 oz., Australia – **$50-60**

ESSO Handy Oil, Esso Standard Oil (Australia) Pty. Ltd., Rect., 4 oz., Australia
$29-38

Oil Company Oilers

ESSO
Handy Oil, Oval, 4 oz.,
Sweden – **$30-50**

ESSO
Handy Oil, Imperial Oil Ltd.,
Oval, 4 oz., Canada
(silver color) – **$25-36**

ESSO
Handy Oil, "Happy"
the Oil Drop Man, 3 oz.
$38-48

ESSO Handy Oil, Esso
Standard, Rect., 4 oz.,
France (front view) – **$60-75**

ESSO
(back view)

EXXON
Universal Oil, Rect., 100 ml.,
Germany – **$25-40**

EXXON
Universal öl, Rect., 100ml.,
Germany, "Replicated"
$22-32

FAR-GO
Machine Oil, Fargo
Company, Oval, 1 oz.,
very scarce – **$80+**

FINA
All Purpose Lubricant, 1/2 oz.,
complimentary sample,
Canada – **$8-12**

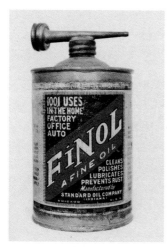

FINOL
A Fine Oil, Standard Oil Co.
of Indiana, Rnd., 8 oz.
$40-60

FINOL
A Fine Oil, Standard Oil Co.,
Rnd., 4 oz., paper label
$27-34

FINOL
A Fine Oil, Standard Oil Co.
of Indiana, Oval, 4 oz.
$35-47

FINOL
A Fine Oil,
Standard Oil Co., 6 oz.
$19-30

FINOL
Household Oil,
Standard Oil Co., Rect., 4 oz.
$18-25

FLEET-WING Household
Oil, Fleet-Wing Corporation,
Rnd., 3 oz., semi-scarce
$29-40

GETTY
Household Oil,
Rect., 4 oz.
$30-40

GOLDEN FLEECE
Home Lubricant, Rect.,
4 oz., Australia
$40-60

GULFOIL A Good Domestic
Lubricant, Gulf Refining Co.,
Oval, 3 oz., circa 1920s, extremely
scarce (front view) – **$400+**

GULFOIL
Price: 30 cents, (back view)

GULFOIL A Good Domestic
Lubricant, Oval, 3 oz., circa
1929, Price: 30 cents,
extremely scarce – **$300-400**

GULFOIL
Store Display Tin for Oiler
circa 1929, extremely scarce
$350+

GULFOIL
Household Lubricant, Short,
wide oval, 4 oz.,
very scarce – **$75+**

GULFOIL A Household Lubri-
cant, 3 oz., circa 1940s, "Free
Sample" sides embossed: "Gulf
Refining Co." very scarce – **$50-70**

GULF
Special Instrument Oil,
Gulf Oil Corp., Rnd., 5cc,
very scarce – **$50-80**

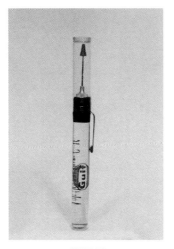

GULF
Rnd., 1/4 oz.
$9-14

HUMBLE
Household Lubricant,
Humble Oil & Refining Co.,
Rect., 4 oz. – **$30-40**

JOHNSON Drop or Two
Oiler, Johnson Refining Co.,
Oval, 4 oz., extremely scarce,
(front view) – **$300+**

JOHNSON
Price: 25 cents
(back view)

KEYSTONE #101 Cutting Oil
2" dia. x 1½" tall reservoir,
sample – paper label, very
scarce (front view) – **$50+**

KEYSTONE
(side view)

KEYSTONE
Penetrating Oil #2
Oval, 3 oz.
$35-45

KEYSTONE
Penetrating Oil #2,
Oval, 1 oz.
$35-45

LEONARD Utility Oil,
Leonard Refineries, Inc.,
Rect. 4 oz., semi-scarce.
$47-57

LINCO
Lincoln Oil Refining, Rnd.,
4 oz., extremely scarce.
$85-120

LINCOIL Lincoln Oil
Refining Co., For General
Household Use, Wide, Oval,
4 oz., extremely scarce – **$150+**

MARATHON
Official All-American Soap
Box Derby Oiler - 1972,
Paper label, scarce – **$50-70**

MARTIN
Machine Oil,
Martin Oil Co., Inc.,
Oval, 3 oz. – **$45-60**

M-F-A
Household Oil, M-F-A Oil
Company, Oval, 3 oz., Made
upside down – **$29-40**

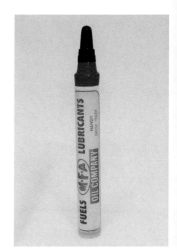

M-F-A
Handy Drop Oiler,
Rnd., 1/2 oz.
$6-10

MFA
Oil, Handy Drop Oiler,
Rnd., 1/2 oz.
$6-10

MID CONTINENT
Household Oil, Mid Continent
Petroleum Corp., Rec., 4 oz.,
very scarce – **$48-70**

MIDOLEUM
Household Oil, The Midland
Refining Co., Rnd., 8 oz.,
very scarce – **$50+**

MIDLAND
Oiler, 3" dia. x 7 1/4" tall
$40-50

MIDLAND
Fine Oil, Midland
Cooperatives, Inc., Obl., 3 oz.
$20-30

MIDLAND
Fine Oil, Obl., 3 oz.
$18-27

MOBILE-GARGOYLE
Handy Oil, Standard-
Vacuum, Oval, 4 oz.,
extremely scarce – **$400+**

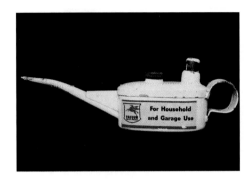

MOBIL
Handy Oil, 7¹/8" long x 1⁵/8" dp. x 2¹/4" tall,
extremely scarce, (front view)
$300+

MOBILE
(back view)

MOBIL
Handy Oil, Socony-Vacuum,
Rect., 8 oz., semi-scarce
$45-65

MOBIL
Handy Oil, Vacuum Oil Co. of
South Africa, Ltd., Rect.,
4 oz., scarce – **$100+**

MOBILBURETTE
(Gargoyle) wide oval, 5 oz.,
France, scarce
$60-80

MOBILBURETTE
wide oval, 5 oz., France,
scarce – **$50-75**

MOBIL
Handy Oil, Rect., 4 oz.
$16-22

MOBIL
Handy Oil, Rect., 4 oz.,
Australia
$28-38

MYSTIK
Household Oil, Cato Oil &
Grease Co., Rect., 4 oz.
$18-28

OIL-WEL Domestic Lubricant,
North Star Oil & Refining Co.,
Ltd., Rnd., 1¹/2 oz., paper label,
very scarce (front view) **$65-85**

OIL-WEL
(back view)

ORONITE Spring Oil Co. of California, Rnd., 16 oz., with 12" spout, very scarce
$80-120

PACIFIC 66
Household Oil, Pacific Petroleums Ltd., Rect., 4 oz., Canada – **$40+**

PAN-AM Household Oil, American Petroleum Corp., Short, Rect., 4 oz., very scarce – **$45-70**

PAN-AM Household Oil, Pan American Petroleum Corp., Short, Rect., 4 oz., scarce – **$40-60**

PARAGON OIL
Household Oil, Paragon Oil Co., Inc., Rect., 4 oz., scarce
$75+

PENN CHAMP
All Purpose Machine Oil, Oval, 3 oz.
$37-50

PENN CHAMP
All Purpose Machine Oil, Rect., 4 oz.
$20-30

WM. PENN
Electric Motor Oil, Canfield Quality Products, Rect., 4 oz.
$28-38

WM. PENN
Electric Motor Oil, Canfield Oil Co., Rect., 4 oz.
$25-35

WM. PENN
Home Oiler, Wm. Penn Laboratories, Rect., 4 oz.
$19-27

PHILLIPS 66
Household Lubricant, Oval, 4 oz., extremely scarce
$100+

— Oil Company Oilers —

PHILLIPS 66
Dripless Penetrating Oil,
Short, Rect., 4 oz.,
very scarce – **$80+**

PHILLIPS 66
Handy Household Oil, Oval,
4 oz., Extremely scarce,
"Replicated" – **$80+**

PHILLIPS 66
Dripless Penetrating Oil,
Short, Rect., 4 oz.,
very scarce –**$60-80**

PHILLIPS 66
Handy Household Oil,
Rect., 4 oz., circa 1940s
$45-65

PHILLIPS 66
Dripless Penetrating Oil,
Rect., 4 oz., circa pre-1963
$23-30

PHILLIPS 66
Dripless Penetrating Oil,
Rect., 4 oz., circa 1963-73
$20-25

PURE
Household Oil,
The Pure Oil Co., Rect., 4 oz.
$38-52

PURE-SURE
Dripless Oil,
Short, rect., 4 oz.
$39-48

PURITAN-OILS-EM-ALL
Home Lubricant, Rnd., 4 oz.,
extremely scarce, (front view)
$300+

PURITAN-OILS-EM-ALL
(side view)

QUAKER STATE OIL-WEL
Rnd., 1½ oz., paper label,
circa 1920s-30s,
extremely scarce – **$125+**

QUAKER STATE OIL-WEL
& box, Rnd., 1½ oz., paper
label, circa 1920s-30s,
extremely scarce – **$150+**

RED INDIAN HOMOIL
McColl-Frontenac Oil Co. Ltd.,
Rect., 4 oz., circa 1940, Canada,
extremely scarce – **$400+**

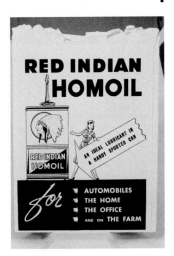

RED INDIAN HOMOIL
Advertisement, circa 1940

RED LINE
Dieso-Life 30,
Union Oil Co., 4 oz.
$29-36

RICHFIELD
Household Oil, Oval, 4oz.,
very scarce
$100+

RPM
Handy Oil, The California
Oil Co., Oval, 3 oz., scarce
$50-75

RPM
Handy Oil, Standard Oil Co.
of California, Rect., 4 oz.
$30-45

RPM
Handy Oil, Standard Oil Co.
of California, Rect., 4 oz.
$18-25

**SKELLY OIL CO.
LABORATORIES**
Oilsall Household Oil, Oval,
4 oz., very scarce – **$80+**

SHELL
Lubricant, Shell Company,
Oval, 3 oz., circa 1928,
extremely scarce –**$250+**

SHELL
Handy Oil, Shell Petroleum
Corp., oval, 3 oz., circa 1930s
very scarce – **$85+**

SHELL
Lubrifiant Domestique, Rect., 8 oz.,
soldered seams, France, very scarce
$70-100

SHELL
Household Oil, Wide Oval,
8 oz., Australia, very scarce
$70-100

SHELL
Household Oil, Rect., 4 oz.,
Australia, very scarce
$70-90

SHELL
Household Oil, Rect., 8 oz.,
New Zealand, scarce
$40-60

SHELL
Lubricant, Oval,
3 oz., scarce
$50-90

SHELL Lubricating Oil,
Specially Recommended for
Tri-ang Trains, 3/4" sq. x
1 11/16 tall, scarce – **$23-34**

SHELL
Household Oil, Wide
Oval, 8 oz. Australia
$75-100

SHELL
Household Oil,
Rect., 4 oz., Australia
$60-70

SHELL
Handy Oil, Oval, 4 oz.,
circa 1940s
$45-55

SHELL
Handy Oil, Rect., 4 oz.
$38-48

SHELL 1948 Soap Box
Derby Lubricant, Rect., 4 oz.,
with paper dealer label,
very scarce – **$75-100**

SHELL Tellus Oil,
Recommended for high speed
bearings, Rect., 4 oz., Canada,
very scarce – **$75+**

SHELL
Household Oil,
Oval, 4 oz., France
$65-80

SHELL
Household Oil, Rect.,
4 oz., circa 1954, Canada
$60-75

SHELL Lubricating Oil,
Specially recommended for
Scalextric Model Cars, 3/4" sq.
x 1 11/16" tall, scarce –**$18-29**

SHELL
Household Oil, 2 oz.,
plastic, Sweden
$30-50

SHELL
Oiler, 120 cc. Plastic,
Sweden
$30-50

SHELL
Oiler, 1 oz., plastic, Sweden
$30-50

SHELL
Handy Oil, 4 oz., plastic,
England – **$40-55**

SHELL Lubricating Oil,
Specially recommended for
Scalextric Model Cars, 3/4" sq.
x 1 11/16" tall, scarce – **$18-29**

SHELL
Household Oil, Rect.,
4 oz., Australia
$50-60

SHELL
Household Oil, Rect.,
4 oz., Australia
$40-60

SHELL
Qualitats Ol, Oval, 100 ml.,
with bar-code, Germany
$30-45

SHELL
Handyman Oil, Rect., 114
ml., England, "Replicated"
$25-37

SHELL
Oil for use in Home & Garden,
Rect., 125 ml., England,
"Replicated" – **$22-32**

Oil Company Oilers

SINCLAIR
Household Oil, Oval, 4 oz.,
scarce – **$90+**

SINCLAIR
Household Oil, Rnd., 1/3 oz.,
$10-20

SINCLAIR
Special Penetrating Oil,
Rnd., 1/3 oz.
$10-20

SKELGAS
Handy Oiler, Rnd., 1/2 oz.
$7-12

SKELLY Household Oil,
Oval, 4 oz., circa 1920s-30s,
price: 25 cents (dark blue color),
extremely scarce – **$200+**

SKELLY
General Use Oil, Rect., 4 oz.
$35-50

SOCONY Lubricote Handy
Oil, Socony-Vacuum
Specialties Inc., Oval, 4 oz.,
extremely scarce – **$165+**

SOHIO Household Oil, The
Standard Oil Co., Wide Oval, 4
oz., circa mid 1930s, extremely
scarce (front view) – **$275+**

SOHIO Household Oil
(close-up view) "Household
Searchlight Approved...The
Household Magazine"

SOHIO
Household Oil, The Standard
Oil Co., Oval, 3 oz., circa
1939, scarce – **$75+**

SOHIO
Home Oiler, Sohio
Laboratories, Rect., 4 oz.,
circa 1959-62 – **$27-40**

SOHIO Soap Box Derby Oil,
Rect., 4 oz., paper label over
painted can, circa 1950s-60s,
very scarce – **$75+**

81

SOHIO
Home Oiler, Rect., 4 oz.,
circa 1959-62
$25-35

SOHIO
Home Oiler, Rect., 4 oz.
$25-35

SOHIO
Penetrating Oil,
Rect., 4 oz., circa 1959
$25-35

STANDARD OIL CO.
Electric Cycle Oil, 2⅜" dia. x
4" tall, circa 1895, extremely
scarce, (front view) – **$75+**

STANDARD OIL CO.
Electric Cycle Oil, (side view)

STANDARD OIL CO.
Household Lubricant,
Rnd., 8 oz.
$50-70

STANDARD Household
Lubricant, The Atlantic
Refining Co., Rnd., 4 oz., circa
1920s, very scarce – **$45-65**

STANDARD OIL CO.
Household Lubricant,
Rnd., 4 oz., (front view)
$30-48

(The) STANDARD OIL CO.
(side view)

(The) STANDARD OIL CO.
Lubricating Oil, Rnd.,
4 oz., (front view)
$40-60

(The) STANDARD OIL CO.
(side view)

STANDARD Household
Lubricant, Standard Oil Co.,
of California, Rnd., 4 oz.,
circa 1920s-30s – **$38-48**

Oil Company Oilers

STANDARD Household Lubricant, Standard Oil Co. of New Jersey, Wide Oval, 4 oz., very scarce – **$55-75**

STANDARD Handy Oil, Standard Oil Co. of Canada, 3 oz., Canada **$50-70**

STANDARD OIL Handy Oil, Standard Oil Co. of California, Oval, 3½ oz., circa 1930s-40s, scarce –**$65-85**

STANDARD Handy Oil, Standard Oil Co., of California, Rect., 4 oz., circa 1930s-40s – **$55-75**

SUNOCO Household Oil, Sample, 9/16" dia. x 1¾" tall **$13-20**

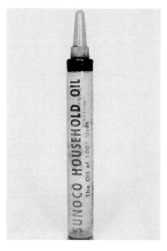

SUNOCO Household Oil, Rnd., ½ oz. **$9-14**

SUNOCO OIL CO. LTD. 14 ml., Canada **$5-10**

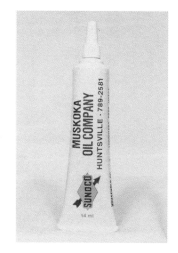

SUNOCO Muskoka Oil Co., 14 ml., Canada **$5-10**

SUNOCO General Purpose Oil, 14 ml., Canada **$5-10**

SUPERTEST Household Oil, Supertest Petroleum Corp. Ltd., Oval, 4 oz., very scarce, "Replicated" – **$90+**

SUPERTEST Utility Oil, Oval, 4 oz., Made upside down, Canada, "Replicated" – **$30-40**

TEXACO Gun Oil The Texas Company, Rect., 16 oz., circa teens-20s, extremely scarce – **$150-200**

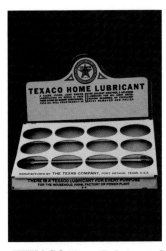

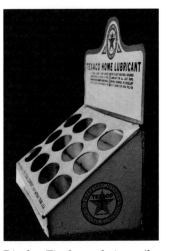

TEXACO
Home Lubricant, Rnd., 8 oz.,
circa teens-20s, extremely
scarce – **$350+**

TEXACO Home Lubricant, Store Display Tin for oval, 4 oz. oil-
ers, 12½" wd. x 5" dp. x 11½ " tall, circa 1920s, extremely scarce.
Left: (Front View)   Right: (Side View)
(The display folds down flat) – **$500+**

TEXACO
Home Lubricant, Texaco
Canada Ltd., Oval, 4 oz.,
scarce – **$65+**

TEXACO
Home Lubricant, Oval, 3 oz.,
Germany – **$38-50**

TEXACO
Home Lubricant,
Rect., 4 oz., Canada
$18-25

TEXACO
Home Lubricant,
Rect., 4 oz., Canada
$18-25

TEXACO
Home Lubricant,
Rect., 4 oz., Canada
$18-25

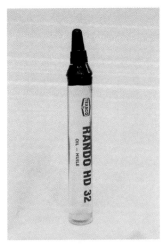

TEXACO
Rando HD 32, Rnd., ½ oz.
$6-9

UNION
Home Lube, Union Oil Co. of
California, Rect., 6½ oz.
copyright 1939 – **$50-70**

UNION
Machine Oil, Obl., 3 oz.,
Copyright 1940
$45-65

VALVOLINE
White Oil, Rect., 3 oz.
(front view)
$35-50

VALVOLINE
White Oil
(back view)

VEEDOL
"sample, 15/8" wd. x 3/4" dp. x
27/8" tall, very scarce
$35-50

VEEDOL
Household Oil, Tidewater
Associated Oil Co., Oval, 4
oz., extremely scarce – **$180+**

VEEDOL
Oval, 4 oz., extremely scarce
$150+

VEEDOL
Household Oil, 4 oz.,
very scarce
$40-60

WANDA
Cream Separator Oil,
Rnd., 16 oz.
$16-22

WHITE ROSE
Handy Oil, 3 oz., scarce
$40-65

WHITE ROSE
Handy Oil, Rnd., 1/2 oz.
$15-25

WOLF'S HEAD
Dripless Penetrating Oil,
Short, Rect., 4 oz.
$30-40

ZEPHYR
Utility Oil, J.D. Streett &
Co., Inc., Rect., 4 oz., circa
1943-63, scarce – **$125+**

OTHER PRODUCTS
(Packaged in the same type of containers as oil)

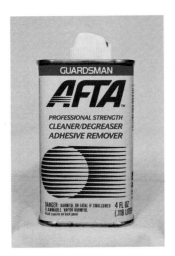

AFTA Cleaner, Degreaser, Adhesive Remover, Guardsman Products, Inc., Rect. 4 oz., circa 1973-on – **$5-10**

ALL AMERICAN
Lighter Fuel, Penn Champ, Inc., Rect., 4 oz., circa 1963-73 – **$17-27**

ALLIED
Lighter Fluid, Allied Drug Products Co., Oval, 4 oz. **$28-36**

AMERICAN FLYER
Track Cleaning Fluid, Oval, 4 oz., paper label, scarce **$30-40**

AMERICAN FLYER
Track Cleaning Fluid, The A.C. Gilbert Co., Rect., 4 oz., paper label – **$30-45**

AMOCO
Lighter Fluid & Spot Remover, American Oil Co., Rect., 4 oz. – **$30-40**

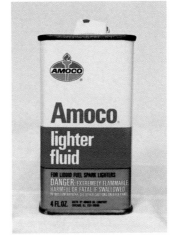

AMOCO
Lighter Fluid, Rect., 4 oz., circa 1963-73 **$10-17**

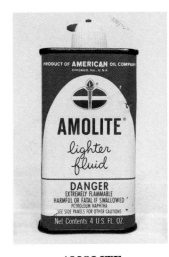

AMOLITE
Lighter Fluid, Rect., 4 oz. **$14-20**

AMOLITE
Lighter Fluid, Rect., 4 oz. **$14-20**

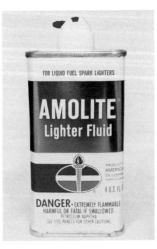

AMOLITE
Lighter Fluid, Rect., 4 oz. **$14-22**

A-M-R Lighter Fuel, A-M-R Chemical Co., Rect., 4 oz. **$25-35**

ASHLAND CHEMICALS
Lighter Fluid, Rect., 4 oz., circa 1963-73 – **$20-30**

OTHER PRODUCTS
(Packaged in the same type of containers as oil)

ATLANTIC Safety – Kleen
The Atlantic Refining Co.,
Rect., 3 oz., scarce
$25-35

ATLANTIC
Lighter Fluid, Rect., 4 oz.
$28-38

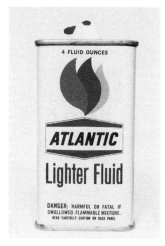

ATLANTIC
Lighter Fluid, Rect., 4 oz.
$17-24

ATOMIC
Lighter Fluid, Dome
Chemical Corp., Rect., 4 oz.,
circa 1950s-63 – **$16-26**

BEL-LITE
Lighter Fluid, Bell Chemical
Co., Oval, 3 oz, paper label,
Price: 15 cents – **$37-50**

B-K
Belt dressing, Rect., 4 oz.
$12-18

BP
Lighter Fluid & Spot
Remover, Rect., 5 oz.,
United Kingdom – **$50-70**

BRUCE
Cleaning Wax, Rect., 4 oz.
$13-20

BRUCE
Floor Cleaner, Rect., 4 oz.
$13-20

CARNU
Oval, 2 oz., sample
$15-24

CENTURY Lighter Fluid,
Twentieth Century Products
Co., Rect., 4 oz. – **$24-34**

CHEVRON
Lighter Fluid, Rect., 4 oz.
$17-25

OTHER PRODUCTS
(Packaged in the same type of containers as oil)

CHEVRON
Lighter Fluid, Rect., 4 oz.,
circa 1963-73

CHRYCO
Lighter Fluid, Rect., 4 oz.,
circa 1966, Canada
$18-30

CITGO
Lighter Fluid, Rect., 4 oz.
$11-17

CITIES SERVICE
Lighter Fluid, Rect., 4 oz.
$50-65

CITIES SERVICE
Lighter Fluid, Rect., 4 oz.,
circa 1950s-60s
$30-40

CITIES SERVICE
Lighter Fluid, Rect., 4 oz.
$14-21

CMC
Lighter Fluid, Obl., 3 oz.
$12-18

COLIBRI
Lighter Fuel,
Oval, 4 oz., Canada
$25-35

COMET Lighter Fluid,
Cardinal Products Co., Inc.,
Rect., 4 oz. – **$17-24**

CONOCO
Lighter Fluid, Continental
Oil Co., Rect., 4 oz. – **$20-30**

CONOCO
Lighter Fluid, Rect., 4 oz.
$18-28

CONOCO
Lighter Fluid, Rect., 4 oz.,
circa 1963-73 – **$13-24**

OTHER PRODUCTS
(Packaged in the same type of containers as oil)

CONOCO
Lighter Fluid, Rect., 4 oz.,
circa 1963-73
$11-22

CO-OP
Lighter Fluid,
Rect., 4 oz.
$12-18

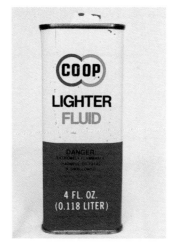

CO-OP
Lighter Fluid, Tall, Obl., 4 oz.
$12-18

CORNELL
Belt Dressing, Cornell Tire
& Rubber Co., Rect., 4 oz.,
circa 1963-73 – **$13-22**

CRISTY
Clear-Glass De-Icer, Cristy
Chemical Corp., Rect., 4 oz.
$20-30

CRISTY
Clear Glass Windshield
De-Icer, Rect., 4 oz.
$18-27

CYCLE Burning Oil,
Vacuum Oil Company Ltd.,
Wide Oval, 7 1/2 oz., scarce,
England –**$60-85**

DAISY HEDDON
Neatsfoot Oil, Rnd., 1.6 oz.
$10-20

DEEP ROCK Lighter
Fluid, A Product of Kerr-
McGee, Rect., 4 oz. – **$38-48**

DERBY Lighter Fluid, The
Derby Oil Co., Oval, 4 oz.,
very scarce – **$75+**

DERBY
Lighter Fluid, Oval, 4 oz.
scarce – **$55-70**

DOUBLE DUTY
Gas Range & Stove Cleanser,
Oval, 4 oz., scarce – **$29-39**

OTHER PRODUCTS
(Packaged in the same type of containers as oil)

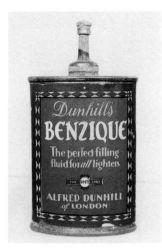

DUNHILL'S
Benzique, Alfred Dunhill
of London, Oval, 2½ oz.,
paper label – **$50-70**

DUNHILL
"Benzique" Lighter Fluid,
Tall, Rect., 5 oz.
$22-34

DU PONT
Speedy Wax, Oval,
3 oz., sample
$12-20

DU PONT
Duco 7 Polish, Oval,
3 oz., sample
$11-18

EL PASO
Red Flame Lighter Fluid, El
Paso Natural Gas Products
Co., Rect., 4 oz. – **$25-35**

ENERGINE Cigar Lighter Fluid,
The Cummer Products Co., 2¼"
dia. x 6" tall, price: 25 cents,
soldered seams, scarce – **$45-65**

ENERGINE
The Perfect Dry Cleaner,
Rnd., 2½ oz.
$15-25

ENERGINE
Cleaning Fluid, Short,
Obl., 3 oz.
$12-18

ENERGINE Lighter Fluid,
The Cummer Co. Div. of Sterling
Drug Inc., Oval, 3 oz. – **$19-28**

ENERGINE Cleaning Fluid,
The Cummer Co., Rect., 4oz.,
circa 1943-63 – **$12-19**

ENERGINE
Lighter Fuel, Rect., 4 oz.,
Price: 25 cents – **$12-18**

ENOZ Cigar Lighter Fluid,
Enoz Chemical Co., Oval, 3
oz., paper label – **$45-55**

Other Products
(Packaged in the same type of containers as oil)

ENOZ
Lighter Fluid, Oval, 3 oz.
$50-65

ESSO Spezial
(Lighter Fluid), oval, 125cm.,
Germany, (front view)
$45-55

ESSO
(back view)

ESSO
Lighter Fluid, Oval,
120 cm., Sweden
$30-50

ESSO
Lighter Fluid, Rect., 4 oz.,
France, (front view)
$65-75

ESSO
(back view)

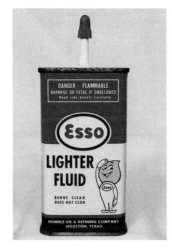

ESSO
Lighter Fluid, Humble Oil &
Refining Co., Rect., 4 oz.
$18-29

ESSO
Tiger Benzin, (Lighter Fluid),
Rect., 125 ml., Germany
$18-26

EVERGLOW
Lighter Fluid, Dome Chemical
Co., Oval, 4 oz. – **$30-40**

EVERGLO
Lighter Fluid, Obl., 3 oz.
$15-25

EVER-READY
Lighter Fluid, Plough, Inc.,
obl., 3 oz. – **$13-23**

EVER-READY Lighter
Fluid, Ever-Ready Co., Obl.,
3 oz., price: 10 cents – **$13-23**

OTHER PRODUCTS
(Packaged in the same type of containers as oil)

EVER-READY
Lighter Fluid, Plough Inc.,
Tall, Obl., 4 oz.
$10-20

EXXON
Lighter Fluid, Rect., 4 oz.
$13-20

FARBO
Cello Wax, The Farbo-Wax
Co., Oval, 3 oz., soldered
seams – **$13-23**

FINA
Lighter Fluid, Rect., 4 oz.
$13-23

FISHER
Auer Lighter Fuel, Oval,
4 oz., Canada
$20-30

FLICK FLASH Lighter
Fuel, By Whiz, Rect., 4 oz.,
(R.M. Hollingshead Corp.)
(dark blue color) – **$25-35**

FLO-MASTER Ink
(yellow) Cushman & Denison
Mfg., Co., Rect., 2 oz.
$14-24

FLO-MASTER
Ink (black), Rect., 4 oz.
$13-24

FLO-MASTER Black Ink,
Esterbrook Pen Co., Rect.,
4 oz., circa 1943-63 – **$13-24**

FLO-MASTER
Black Ink, The Esterbrook
Pen Co., Rect., 4 oz. – **$13-23**

FLO-MASTER
Ink, Venus Esterbrook Corp.,
Rect., 4 oz. – **$13-23**

FLYING-A
Lighter Fluid, Rect., 4 oz.
$35-45

OTHER PRODUCTS

(Packaged in the same type of containers as oil)

FRIGIDAIRE
Surface Renewer, Frigidaire
Div. – General Mtrs. Corp.,
Rect., 4 oz. – **$18-28**

GOODYEAR
Lighter Fluid, Rect., 4 oz.,
circa 1963-73
$16-25

GULF
Lighter Fluid, Rect., 4 oz.
$19-25

GULF
Lighter Fluid,
Oval, 4 oz., Canada
$22-32

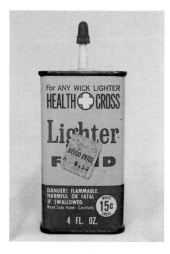

HEALTH CROSS
Lighter Fluid, Rect., 4 oz.,
Price: 12 cents, circa 1963-73
$12-18

HOLLINGSHEAD Vinyl
Top Wax, R.M. Hollingshead
Corp., Rect., 4 oz., circa early
1970s, price: 35 cents – **$20-30**

HOLLINGSHEAD
Old Faithful Lighter Fluid,
Rect., 4 oz.
$20-30

IDEAL
Lighter Fluid, Universal
Chemical Co., Rect., 4 oz.
$20-30

INDIAN Motor Cleaner
Indian Motorcycle Company,
Rect., 4 oz., very scarce – **$70+**

IT LIGHTER FLUID
Rect., 110 ml., (with
bar-code), Canada – **$8-15**

JACK FROST Lighter
Fluid, Jack Frost, Inc., Rect.,
4 oz., scarce – **$60-75**

KEM Paint Brush & Roller
Cleaner, Rect., 4 oz., "Trial
Package" – **$12-19**

OTHER PRODUCTS
(Packaged in the same type of containers as oil)

KERR MCGEE
Lighter Fluid, Rect., 4 oz.,
circa 1963-73
$11-18

KERR MCGEE
Lighter Fluid, Rect., 4 oz.,
$11-18

KEYSTONE
Lighter Fluid, Emblem Oil
Co., Rect., 4 oz.
$23-32

KEYSTONE
Lighter Fluid,
Tall, Rect., 5 oz.
$26-35

KLEAN-CLEAN
Rect., 4 oz.
$7-15

KWIK-LITE-
Radiant, For All Cigarette
Lighters, Midway Chemical
Co., Oval, 4 oz. – **$30-45**

KWIK-LITE
Lighter Fluid, Boyle-Midway
Inc., Tall, Obl., 4 oz.
$18-27

KWIK SOLV
Solvent, Atomized Materials
Co., Inc., Rect., 4 oz.
$12-19

LINDE
Nozzle Compound, Rect., 4 oz.,
paper label – **$14-23**

LIONEL Track Cleaner for
Model Trains, The Lionel
Corp., Oval, 3 oz. – **$30-40**

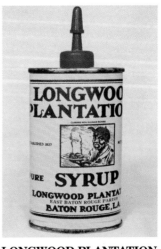

LONGWOOD PLANTATION
Pure Syrup, Oval, 3 oz., paper
label, "Free Sample" – **$20-35**

MAJESTIC Sleetchaser
Fluid, Majestic Products Co.,
Obl., 1 oz. – **$15-25**

OTHER PRODUCTS
(Packaged in the same type of containers as oil)

MARSH
Ink, "Best For All Felt-Point
Pens", Marsh Co., Obl., 1 oz.
$12-22

MARSH
Marker Ink, "Best For All
Felt-Point Pens", Marsh
Stencil, Rect., 4 oz. – **$14-25**

MERCURY Lighter Fuel,
Mercury Products Div. of
A.M.R. Chemical Co.,
Rect., 4 oz. – **$17-27**

MET-LIT
Solvent, Whiz Product –
R.M. Hollingshead Corp.,
Rect., 4 oz. – **$17-27**

MOPAR
Glass Cleaner, Rect., 10 oz.
$23-35

MOTOR OVERHAUL
Pope Chemical Co., Oval,
4 oz., price: $2.98,
circa 1940s-50s – **$18-28**

NAPA – BALKAMP
Lighter Fluid, Rect., 4 oz.
$14-20

NAPA
Belt Dressing, Tall, Rect.,
4 1/2 oz., circa 1963-73
$14-22

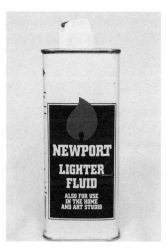

NEWPORT
Lighter Fluid, Tall,
Rect., 4 1/2 oz. – **$9-17**

NO SAND Surface Prepara-
tion, The Kleen Strip Co.,
Rect., 4 oz., "Sample" – **$12-17**

NYLITE
Lighter Fluid, Obl., 1 oz.
$12-18

O.K. CUB Glow Fuel,
Herkimer Tool & Model Works,
Inc., Rect., 4 oz. – **$14-20**

— OTHER PRODUCTS —

OTHER PRODUCTS
(Packaged in the same type of containers as oil)

OLD FAITHFUL
Lighter Fluid, Another
ALL-NU Product, Rect.,
4 oz., scarce –$40-65

OLD FAITHFUL Lighter Fluid,
Universal Chem. Div. – R.M. Hollingshead Corp., Rect., 4 oz., circa
1950s-60s, semi-scarce – **$40-55**

OLYMPIAN
Candle Fuel, Rect., 4 oz.
$15-24

PACIFIC 66
Lighter Fluid, Pacific
Petroleums Ltd., Rect.,
4 oz., Canada – **$40+**

PENN CHAMP
Lighter Fuel, Penn Champ
Oil Corp., Tall, Obl., 4 oz.
$12-22

PENN CHAMP
Lighter Fuel, Rect., 4 oz.,
circa 1973-on, "Package Not
Child Resistant" – **$17-25**

PENN CHAMP
Lighter Fuel, Rect., 4 oz.
$17-25

PENNEYS
Belt Dressing, Rect., 4 oz.,
$17-25

PENN-JERSEY Lighter Fluid,
Penn Jersey Auto Stores, Inc.,
Rect., 4 oz., (front view) – **$30-40**

PENN-JERSEY
(back view)

(The) PEP BOYS
Lighter Fluid, Rect., 4 oz.,
(front view) – **$30-44**

(The) PEP BOYS
(back view)

(The) PEP BOYS
Lighter Fluid, Rect., 4 oz.,
(front view)
$30-44

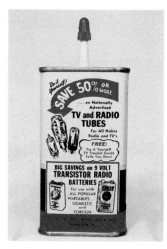

(The) PEP BOYS
(back view)

PEP-MO Tune-Up Recondi-
tioner, Trilla Products, Inc.,
Oval, 4 oz., paper label, circa
1943-early 50s – **$20-30**

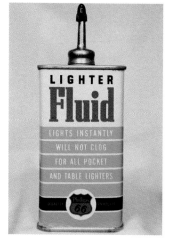

PHILLIPS 66
Lighter Fluid, Rect., 4 oz.
$35-45

PHILLIPS 66
Lighter Fluid, Rect., 4 oz.,
circa pre-1963
$15-22

PHILLIPS 66
Lighter Fluid, Rect., 4 oz.,
circa 1963-73
$10-17

PLASTIC WOOD
Solvent, Boyle-Midway Co.,
Oval, 3 oz., circa 1943-63
$12-19

PLASTIC WOOD
Solvent Boyle-Midway Co.,
Wide, Oval, 3 oz.
$13-20

PLASTIC WOOD
Solvent, 3-IN-ONE Product,
Rect., 4 oz., circa 1967 – **$12-17**

PLASTIC WOOD Solvent,
3-IN-ONE Product, Rect., 4
oz., circa 1973-on – **$8-16**

PURE-SURE
Lighter Fluid, Rect., 4 oz.
$40-60

PURE
Lighter Fluid, Rect., 4 oz.
$30-45

Other Products
(Packaged in the same type of containers as oil)

RED DEVIL'S Lighter Fluid, Devil Laboratories Co., Oval, 4 oz., circa 1940s, price: 15 cents, very scarce –**$70+**

RED DEVIL'S Lighter Fluid, Dome Chemical Corp., Rect., 4 oz., circa 1950s-63 – **$20-27**

RED DEVIL Lighter Fluid, Red Devil Products, Inc., Rect., 4¹/² oz., circa 1973-on – **$9-14**

RED DEVIL Lighter Fluid, Rect., 4¹/² oz., circa 1973-on **$5-12**

REGENT Baseball Glove Conditioner, Tall, Rect., 4 oz., circa 1973-on - **$13-22**

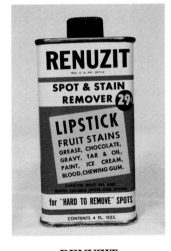

RENUZIT Spot & Stain Remover, Rect., 4 oz., circa 1943-63, price: 29 cents – **$12-19**

RENUZIT Spot Remover, Rect., 4 oz., circa 1943-63, "With Free Applier" – **$14-22**

RICHFIELD Lighter Fluid, Rect., 4 oz. **$27-38**

RONSONAL Lighter Fuel, Ronson Art Metal Works (Canada) Ltd., Oval, 4 oz., "Replicated" – **$25-35**

RONSONAL Jiffy-Fill, (One time lighter re-fill), 1/8" wd. x 7/16" dp. x 2¹/4" tall, plastic – **$5-10**

ROZ-IN-IZE Shoe & Leather Dressing, "Used & Endorsed by Admiral Byrd's Antarctic Expeditions", Rect., 4 oz. – **$14-24**

RUBYFLUID Soldering & Tinning Flux, The Ruby Chemical Co., Oval, 3 oz., (dark blue color) – **$30-45**

OTHER PRODUCTS
(Packaged in the same type of containers as oil)

RU-GLYDE
Tire'n Mat Dressing,
Rect., 8 oz.
$17-22

RUSTOP
Whiz – R.M. Hollingshead
Corp., Oval, 1³/₄ oz.
$18-25

SANFORD'S
Dri Line Ink, Sanford Ink
Co., Oval, 4 oz.
$28-38

SAPO Lighter Fluid, Sapo
Elixir Chemical Co., Oval,
4 oz., price: 30 cents, circa
1930s-40s – **$25-37**

SCHALK
Wood Filler Solvent, Rect.,
4 oz., paper label
$12-19

SEARS
Belt Dressing, Rect., 4 oz.,
circa: pre-1963
$16-27

SEARS
Belt, Leather & Rubber
Dressing, Rect., 4 oz.
$15-24

SELF STARTING
Lighter Fluid, The New
Method Mfg., Co., Oval, 2 oz.,
very scarce – **$35-55**

SHAMROCK
Lighter Fluid, Rect., 4 oz.
$20-30

SHELL Junior For Cleaning & Automatic
Lighters, Shell-Max & B.P. Ltd., 3¹/₄" wd. x
1⁷/₈" dp. x 3⁷/₈" tall reservoir, soldered
seams, Australia, very scarce – **$60-80**

SHELL Junior For Cleaning & Automatic
Lighters, Shell-Max & B.P. Ltd., 3¹/₄" wd. x
1⁷/₈" dp. x 3⁷/₈" tall reservoir, soldered seams,
Australia, very scarce – **$60-80**

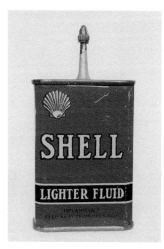

SHELL
Lighter Fluid, Rect., 4 oz.,
Australia – **$60-75**

Other Products
(Packaged in the same type of containers as oil)

SHELL
Lighter & Cleaning Fluid,
Rect., 4 oz., Australia
$60-70

SHELL
Lighter Fluid, Oval, 3½ oz.,
scarce, (front view)
$60-80

SHELL
Cleaning Fluid
(back view)

SHELL
Lighter Fluid, Oval, 4 oz.
$75-90

SHELL
Lighter Fluid, Rect., 4 oz.
$50-70

SHELL
(Junior) Lighter Fluid &
Spot Remover, Rect., 5 oz.,
England – **$40-60**

SHELL
Lighter Fluid, Rect., 4 oz.,
circa 1950s
$40-60

SHELL
Lighter Fluid & Spot
Remover, Rect., 4 oz.,
circa pre-1963 – **$20-30**

SHELL
Lighter Fluid, Rect., 4 oz.,
circa pre-1963 – **$20-30**

SHELL
Fluid & Spot Remover, Rect.,
4 oz., circa pre-1963 – **$20-30**

SHELL
Fluid & Spot Remover, Rect.,
4 oz., Australia – **$40-55**

SHELL
Lighter Fluid 4 oz., plastic,
Sweden, scarce – **$30-50**

100

Other Products

(Packaged in the same type of containers as oil)

SHELL
Lighter Fluid,
Rect., 4 oz., Australia
$40-50

SHELL
Lighter Fluid & Spot
Remover, Rect., 8 oz.,
circa 1963-73 – **$17-22**

SHELL Reines Benzin
(Lighter Fluid), Oval, 125
ml., Germany, "replicated"
$30-45

SHELL Reines Benzin
(Lighter Fluid), Tall, Rect.,
125 ml., Germany (with
bar-code) – **$25-40**

SHUR-FYRE
Pocket Lighter Fluid,
Distributed by Peoples Drug
Stores, Oval, 3 oz. – **$35-50**

SINCLAIR
Lighter Fluid, Oval, 4 oz.
$35-45

SKELLY
Lighter Fluid, Rnd., 8 oz.
$30-40

SOHIO
Lighter Fluid, The Standard
Oil Co., of Ohio, Rect., 4 oz.
$30-45

SOHIO Lighter Fluid, Sohio
Laboratories, Rect., 4 oz.
$23-30

SOHIO Lighter Fluid,
Rect., 4 oz., circa 1950s-
early 60s – **$23-30**

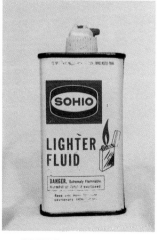

SOHIO Lighter Fluid,
Rect., 4 oz., circa 1965
$25-33

SOHIO
Lighter Fluid, Tall, Rect.,
4 1/2 oz. – **$25-33**

Other Products

(Packaged in the same type of containers as oil)

SOLITE
Lighter Fluid, American Oil
Co., Rect., 4 oz.
$14-23

SPEEDMASTER Marking
Pen Ink, Certified Metal
Products, Rect., 4 oz., paper
label, circa 1950s-60s – **$14-24**

SPITFIRE
Lighter Fluid, Robinson &
Webber Ltd., Oval, 4 oz.,
Canada – **$25-35**

SPOKTITE Tightens Loose
Wheels, The Woodtite Laboratories,
Oval, 3 oz., (painted label), circa
1920s-30s, very scarce – **$60-90**

SPREADER-STICKER
Obl., 1 oz.
$11-17

STANDARD
Garden Spray, Rect., 4 oz.
$20-30

STARLITER Fluid,
(Lighter Fluid), Potomac
Corporation, Obl., 1 oz.
$15-24

SUNOCO
Lighter Fluid, Rect., 4 oz.,
(dark blue color), (front view)
$20-30

SUNOCO
Lighter Fluid, (back view)

SUNOCO
Lighter Fluid, Rect., 4 oz.,
(front view) – **$14-22**

SUNOCO
Lighter Fluid
(back view)

SUPER LIGHT Lighter
Fluid, The Union News
Company, Rect., 4 oz., – **$25-35**

OTHER PRODUCTS
(Packaged in the same type of containers as oil)

SURE FIRE
Lighter Fuel, Wilco Co.,
Rect., 4 oz.
$10-16

SUR-FLAME
Lighter Fluid, The Arctic
Sur-Flow Co., Tall, Obl., 4
oz., Canada – **$19-28**

SURE-LIGHT The Perfect Filling
Fluid For all Lighters, Marine
Laboratories, Oval, 3 oz., (paper
label), (dark blue color) – **$30-48**

TAVERN
Non-Rub Floor Wax,
Socony-Vacuum Oil Co.,
Oval, 4 oz., "Sample" – **$50+**

TAVERN
Paint Cleaner, Oval, 4 oz.,
"Sample" – **$50+**

TAVERN
Stain Remover, (for
varnished surfaces), Oval,
3 oz., scarce – **$30-45**

TESTORS
Lighter Fluid, Tall, Obl.,
4 oz., price: 25 cents
$18-28

TEXACO
Lighter Fluid, Oval, 125 cm.,
(with dark blue), circa 1967,
Sweden – **$30-50**

TEXACO Lighter Fluid,
Rect., 4 oz., circa late 1960s,
Canada – **$14-22**

TEXTONE
Fabric Cleaner, Rect., 4 oz.,
copyright 1954 – **$12-19**

TEXTONE Leather &
Plastic Cleaner, Rect., 4 oz.,
copyright 1954 – **$12-19**

TREWAX Tre Bien Furniture Cream,
Trewax Mfg. Co., of the Midwest, Inc.,
Rect., 4 oz., "Sample" – **$12-19**

Other Products

(Packaged in the same type of containers as oil)

TREWAX
Gold Label Floor Wax,
Rect., 4 oz., "Sample"
$12-19

TREWAX
Floor Cleaner, Rect.,
4 oz., "Sample"
$12-19

TREWAX
Liquid Floor Wax, Rect.,
4 oz., "Sample"
$12-19

TREWAX
Wax Stripper, Rect., 4 oz.,
"Sample" – **$12-19**

TREWAX
Tre Bien Lemon Oil
Furniture Cream, Rect.,
4 oz., "Sample" – **$12-19**

TRI-CHEM
E-Z Flo Tip Cleaner &
Solvent, Rect., 4 oz,., paper
label, circa 1963-73 – **$13-18**

TRIOGEN
A Rose Spray, The Rose Mfg.
Co., Oval, 4 oz.
$19-29

TRIOGEN
A Rose Spray, Rect., 4 oz.
$17-24

UNION
Lighter Fluid, Rect., 4 oz.,
circa 1963-73 – **$15-20**

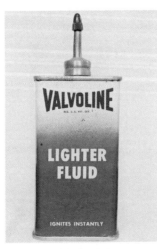

VALVOLINE
Lighter Fluid, Rect., 4 oz.
$33-44

WALGREENS
Lito Lighter Fluid, Rect., 4
oz., circa 1963-73 – **$13-22**

WALLIN FOSTER ASSOC.
Auto Motor Heater Primer
Fuel, Rect., 4 oz. – **$33-50**

Other Products

(Packaged in the same type of containers as oil)

WESTERN AUTO
Lighter Fluid, Rect., 4 oz.
$16-24

S.S. WHITE
Cleaner, The S.S. White
Dental Mfg. Co., Rect., 4 oz.,
paper label – **$28-37**

WOOD-N-STREAM
Dressing for Boots & Shoes,
Albert H. Weinbrenner Co.,
Obl., 1 oz. – **$11-16**

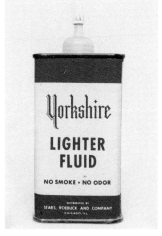

YORKSHIRE
Lighter Fluid, Sears,
Roebuck & Co., Rect., 4 oz.
$19-29

ZAIGER
De-Icer Fluid, Obl., 1 oz.
$16-25

ZIPPO
Lighter Fuel, Tall, Rect.,
5oz., price: 29 cents
$11-17

ZIPPO
Lighter Fluid, Tall, Rect.,
4 1/2 oz.
$7-11

ZIPPO
Lighter Fluid, 65 Year
Anniversary Can, Tall, Rect.,
4 1/2 oz., circa 1997 – **$7-10**

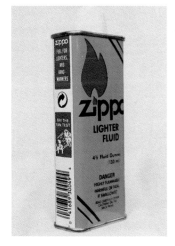

ZIPPO
Lighter Fluid, Tall, Rect.,
4 1/2 oz., circa 1973-on – **$7-10**

ANTAR Essence Pour
Briquets, (Lighter Fluid),
Oval, 4 oz., France – **$35-45**

ADLER
Rect., 4 oz.
$25-35

AMR
Rect., 4 oz.
$15-24

APPROVED
Rect., 4 oz.
$11-16

S.F. BAKER & CO. Extra Fine
Machine Oil, "Prepared
Expressly for Sewing Machine
Use" 6 oz., price 35 cents – **$23-33**

BAKER'S
Machine Oil, 6 oz.,
price 35 cents
$20-28

BAKERS
Machine Oil, 6 oz.
$13-20

BEE BRAND
McCormick & Co., 1 3/8 oz.,
scarce – **$17-27**

BLEACHED
Sperm Oil, 4 oz.,
circa pre-1910, very scarce
$35-45

"BOYE"
Oil, The Boye Needle Co.,
Oval, 1 oz., – **$25-37**

"BOYE"
Stainless Oil, Oval, 3 oz.
$25-35

"BOYE"
Stainless High Grade Oil,
3 oz. – **$20-29**

BOYE
Stainless Oil, Obl.,
3 oz., price 30 cents
$15-20

BOYE
Stainless Oil, Obl., 3 oz.,
price 45 cents
$15-20

BROTHER
Obl., 3 oz.
$14-27

BUFFALO
Prairie City Oil Co., Rnd.,
4 oz., Canada, Extremely
scarce – **$100+**

CAPO
The Capo Polishes Ltd.,
Oval, 3 oz., Canada
$29-40

CARNATION
Carnation Toilet Co., 3 oz.
$22-30

CHAMBERLAIN'S
Chamberlain Medicine Co.,
2 oz., with box
$27-34

DOMESTIC Continental
Oil Co., 2½" dia. x 2³/₈" tall
reservoir, soldered seams,
Canada, very scarce – **$80+**

DOMESTIC
Haney-Pistor Co., 4 oz.
$35-48

DOMESTIC
Rect., 4 oz.
$22-30

EATON'S
The T. Eaton Co., 4oz.,
circa 1930s, scarce
$30-40

EXCELSIOR Wm. F. Nye,
Triangular – 2" wd. x 5" tall, circa
late 1800s-1910, extremely scarce
(front view)– **$75-100**

EXCELSIOR
(close-up view)

EXCELSIOR
3 oz.
$23-32

FAMOUS
A.F. Wilson, Sewing Machine
Supplies, 3 oz.
$18-28

FISCHER
A.J. Hilbert & Co., 2 oz.
$9-18

FREE
Free Sewing Machine Co.,
Oval, 4 oz.
$19-26

FREE-WAY
Free Sewing Machine Co.,
Obl., 1 oz.
$12-19

FREE-WESTINGHOUSE
Free Sewing Machine Co.,
Rect., 4 oz., semi-scarce
$45-65

GILBERT'S
Gilbert Bros. & Co.,
Wholesale Druggists, 3 oz.
$22-30

GOLDEX
Robinson & Webber, 2 oz.
$9-14

HOUSEHOLD
Obl., 3 oz.
$12-18

IDEAL
Classic Chemical Co.,
Rect., 4 oz.
$14-22

INFACT
Oval, 3 oz., paper label,
Canada – **$17-28**

JPH
J.P. Hadesman & Co., 3 oz.
$28-37

Sewing Machine Oilers

KENMORE
Sears, Roebuck & Co.,
2 oz., (gold label)
$11-16

KENMORE
Obl., 3 oz.
$14-24

F.W. McNESS'
Furst-McNess
Company, 4 oz.
$15-24

MONTGOMERY WARD
Obl., 1 oz.
$12-18

NASCO
National Specialty Co., 4 oz.
$11-17

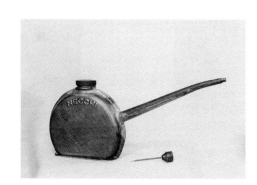

NECCHI
4 3/4" long x 1/2" dp. x 1 3/4" tall,
brass, soldered seams, Italy
$12-20

NECCHI-ELNA
Oval, 3 oz.
$16-25

NECCHI-ALCO
Rect., 4 oz.
$10-19

NEW HOME
W.A. Sweetland, 2 oz.,
extremely scarce
$60+

NEW HOME
Oval, 4oz., scarce
$50-70

NYE'S
Wm. F. Nye, 2 oz., scarce
$30-45

SEWING MACHINE OILERS

O.K.'s OIL
Rect., 4 oz., (dark
blue color), circa 1963-73
$18-28

PANEF
Rect., 4 oz.
$13-18

PENNEYS
Rect., 4 oz., price 30 cents
$18-25

PENNYS
Rect., 4 oz., circa 1963-73,
price 30 cents
$18-28

J.C. PENNEY
Rect., 4 oz., circa 1963-73,
price 45 cents
$13-22

PFAFF
Oval 150 cc, Dutch, scarce
$45-65

PFAFF
Oval, 3 oz., (dark brown
color), Germany
$28-38

PFAFF
Obl., 100 ml., Germany
$18-29

PFAFF
Oiler, 2¼" dia. x 6½" tall,
plastic – **$15-20**

PFAFF
Rect., 4 oz.
$14-20

PFAFF
Rect., 4 oz.
$14-20

PIONEER
Pioneer Tea Co., 4 oz.
$18-26

RAWLEIGH'S
The W.T. Rawleigh Co., Ltd.,
3 oz., Canada
$10-15

RICCAR
Rect., 4 oz.
$15-21

SEAMSTRESS
Rect., 4 oz.
$15-24

SEWING MACHINE OIL
Nith Valley Laboratories,
3 oz., Canada
$28-40

SEWING MACHINE OIL
Oval, 1 1/3 oz.
$20-30

SEWING MACHINE OIL
Oval, 1 1/2 oz.
$22-33

SEWING MACHINE OIL
Rect., 4 oz., circa 1950s
$20-30

SEWING MACHINE OIL
Rect., 4 oz.
$17-26

SEWING MACHINE OIL
Obl., 3 oz.
$13-22

SEWING MACHINE OIL
1 oz., glass bottle
$4-10

SEWLUBE
Obl., 3 oz.
$15-24

SHEPPARD'S
3 oz.
$12-17

SINGER
1⅝" wd. x 1 1/16" dp.
x 3⅝" tall, (oldest found?)
$15-20

SINGER
3 oz.
$20-29

SINGER
3 oz.
$20-29

SINGER
2" wd. x 1¼" dp. x 3" tall,
Spanish, (front view)
$35-50

SINGER
(back view)

SINGER
1⅞" wd. x 1¼" dp. x 3" tall,
Dutch/French, (front view)
$35-50

SINGER
(back view)

SINGER
(and others), By Del-Mar-Va
Sales Co., 1 oz.
$10-17

SINGER
Oval, 1⅓ oz., Great Britain
$22-33

SINGER
3 oz., Spanish
$23-32

SINGER
Oval, 3 oz., Great Britain
$18-28

SINGER
Rect., 4 oz., price 39 cents
$13-20

SINGER
Rect., 4 oz., Canada
$13-20

SINGER
Rnd., 1/2 oz.
$6-10

SINGER
Rnd., 1/2 oz.
$6-10

SPAULDING'S
Spaulding Products Co.,
3 oz.
$18-26

SPERM
Sewing Machine Oil, Bridges-McDowell Co.,
2 1/2" dia. x 4" tall, circa turn of the century, extremely scarce.
(front view)   **$35-55**   (back view)

SPERMOILA
The Bacorn Company, 3 oz.
$10-20

STAINLESS
Oval, 1 1/2 oz.
$22-33

STAINLESS
2 oz.
$9-14

SUPERIOR
Herman Chemical Co.,
3 oz., circa pre-1910,
very scarce – **$35-55**

SUPERIOR
4 oz.
$14-22

TERRIFF'S
Wolverine Soap Co.,
Perfumers, Extract Makers,
2 1/2 oz., very scarce – **$30-45**

VAN OGDEN'S
4 oz.
$24-34

WARD'S
The Ward Company, 4 oz.
$23-30

WARDS
Montgomery Ward,
Oval, 1 oz.
$22-33

WATKINS
J.R. Watkins Medical Co.,
4 1/2 oz.
$15-25

WATKINS
4 1/2 oz.
$10-16

WHITE (front view)
White Sewing Machine Co.,
"The White is King", 3 oz.,
very scarce – **$25-35**

WHITE
(close-up view)

WHITE
3 oz.
$23-32

WHITE
Oval, 4 oz.
$30-40

WHITE
Rect., 4 oz.
$20-30

WHITE
3 oz.
$19-26

WHITE
4 oz., price 25 cents
$9-14

Sewing Machine Oilers

WILDMAN'S
W.H. Wildman & Sons, 8 oz.
$10-17

WILLCOX & GIBBS
Oval, 3 oz., semi-scarce
$40-60

WOOD'S, N. Wood & Son,
1-2 oz., embossed on back:
Estab. 1843, circa mid-late
1800s, very scarce – **$30-50**

Special Purpose Oilers

A-M-R
Bicycle Oil, Oval,
4 oz., scarce
$85+

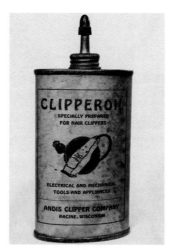

ANDIS
Clipperoil, Andis Clipper Co.,
Oval, 3 oz., paper label
$18-29

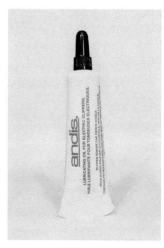

ANDIS
Electric Clipper Oil, ¼ oz.
$.50-1.00

Special Purpose Oilers

AUTO-SOLER OIL
The Auto-Soler Co., Oval,
4 oz., circa 1930s-40s, scarce,
(front view) – **$35-48**

AUTO-SOLER
(close-up view)

BENDIX
High Temperature Breaker
Lubricant, Rect., 4 oz.
$18-28

BESTOIL Cycle Lubricating
Oil, Curran Oils Ltd., Oval, 4
oz., soldered seams, Great
Britain, scarce – **$35-50**

BICYCLE OIL
Blelock Mfg. Co., 1⁵/₈" wd. x
1⁵/₁₆" dp. x 4³/₄" tall, extremely scarce, (front view) – **$75+**

BICYCLE OIL
(close-up view)

BOYER
Electric Motor Oil, Rect.,
8 oz., circa 1950s-60s
$10-18

J.W. BRESSLER'S
Lightning Slide Trombone
Oil, 1¹/₄" dia. x 3¹/₈" tall
$8-14

BUESCHER
Valve Oil, Buescher Band
Instrument Co., Sq., 1 oz.,
price 35 cents – **$7-12**

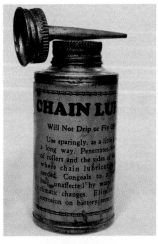

CHAIN LUBE
Easy Shift Products, 1³/₄"
dia. x 3" tall reservoir, circa
early 1940s – **$23-33**

CHAIN LUBE
The McGlaughlin Oil Co.,
Rnd., 4 oz., circa 1950s-
early 60s – **$18-28**

CHEMICO
Cycle Lubricating Oil, Wide
Oval, 7¹/₂ oz., England
$40-48

Special Purpose Oilers

CONN
Key Oil, C.G. Conn, Ltd.,
Sq., 1 oz., price 25 cents
$10-16

CONN
Slide Oil, Sq., 1 oz.,
price 30 cents
$10-16

CONN
Polished Oil, Sq., 1 oz.
$10-16

CONNOR Quality Washers,
J.H. Connor & Son Ltd., Rnd.,
4 oz., w/ 5½" spout, Canada,
very scarce, (front view) – **$75+**

CONNOR
(side view)

CROSS COUNTRY
Special Refrigerator Motor
Oil, Sears, Roebuck & Co.,
Oval, 3 oz., scarce – **$48-70**

CYCLE
Tune-Up, Eezox Inc., Rect.,
4 oz., circa 1973-on
$22-30

DART
Heavy Duty Motor Oil, The
Slick-Shine Co., 5 oz.
$15-18

DE LAVAL
Cream Separator Oil, Rnd.,
8 oz., paper label
$25-35

DIE LUBRICANT
C-H Die Co., Rnd., 2 oz.
$3-6

DIXON'S Spring Oil & Rust
Solvent, Joseph Dixon
Crucible Company, Oval, 3 oz.
$30-40

DRI SLIDE
Bike Aid, Rect., 4 oz.
$15-25

DUCKHAMS
Home Oil / Cycl Oil, Rect.,
4.4 oz., England (front view)
$30-40

DUCKHAMS
(back view)

DUMORE
Cool Bearing Oil, Dumore
Company Inc., Oval, 3 oz.,
paper label – **$25-35**

DUMORE
Ball Bearing Oil, Oval,
3 oz., paper label
$23-30

ELECTRIC
Motor Oil, Western Motor
Service, 1 3/4" dia. x 3" tall
reservoir, paper label – **$15-24**

(Oil For) **ELECTRIC
SHAVERS**
1 5/8" wd. x 11/16" dp. x 2 3/8"
tall, glass bottle – **$6-13**

OILER (Electric Sprayer),
Oval, 3 oz., scarce
$30-42

EMERSON Motoroil, The
Emerson Electric Mfg. Co.,
Rnd., 4 oz., circa 1920s, very
scarce – **$40-60**

EVERYMANS
Cycle Oil, C.C. Wakefield &
Co., Ltd., Wide Oval, 7 1/2 oz.,
England, scarce – **$75+**

"EXCELENE"
Cycle Lubricating Oil, The
Humber Oil Co., Oval, 7 1/2 oz.,
England, scarce – **$75+**

"EXCELENE"
Cycle Lubricating Oil, Oval,
4 oz., England, very scarce
$85+

FARM MASTER
Pulsator Oil, Sears, Roebuck
& Co., Rect., 4 oz.
$25-38

GC
Radio Dial Oil, General
Cement Mfg. Co., Sq., 2 oz.
$12-22

GOMCO
Oil, Oval, 4 oz.,
(silver & dark blue colors)
$26-34

GOMCO
Oil, Rect., 4 oz.
$20-29

GRAMOPHONE OIL
T. Eaton Co., 3 oz., Canada
$9-16

HANDI LUBE
Speedometer Cable
Lubricant, Rnd., 1/2 oz.
$8-12

(The) HENLEY SKATE
2 1/4" dia. x 1/2" dp. x 3 5/8" tall,
(engraved picture of roller
skate), very scarce – **$75+**

HIAWATHA
Harvester Oil, Farwell Ozmun
Kick & Co., 3" dia. x 7 1/2"
tall, very scarce – **$65-90**

(The) HOBART MFG. CO.
Lubricating Oil,
Rnd., 4 oz., circa 1930s
$40-60

HOLTONS
Electric Oil, 1 1/4" dia. x
3 1/4" tall – no label
$7-10

HOLTON
Electric Oil, Rnd., 1 oz.,
paper label, price 25 cents
$5-10

HOLTON
Valve Oil, Frank Holton &
Co., Rnd., 1 oz., painted label
$6-11

HOLTON
New Electric Oil, Rnd., 1 oz.,
paper label, price 35 cents
$5-10

(The) HOOVER
Suction Sweeper Co., Rnd.,
1½ oz., paper label, circa
1920s-30s – **$15-24**

HUSQVARNA
For Mincers, Food Choppers,
Coffee Mills, Rect., 4 oz.,
Sweden, (front view) – **$30-42**

HUSQVARNA
Sewing Machine Oil
(back view)

KANT-RUST
Junior-Spring Lubricant,
Oval, 3 oz., price 30 cents,
extrememly scarce – **$70+**

KING
Valve Oil No. 14, The H.N.
White Co., Rnd., 1 oz.
$7-14

LUBRICATING OIL for
"His Masters Voice" Gramo-
phones, The Gramophone Co.,
Ltd., 1 oz., very scarce – **$30-45**

MARVEL
Air-Tool Oil, Tall Rect., 4 oz.
$13-19

MATHER Thousand Mile Axle
Oil, The Commercial Oil Co., 3½"
wd./ x 1¾" dp. x 6¼" tall, circa
1900, price 25 cents, soldered
seams, extremely scarce – **$120+**

W.A. MAURER
Grounding Oil, 15 cc
$4-10

MAYTAG
Turbine Oil, 4 oz., plastic
$8-12

MEAD CYCLE CO.
Bicycle Oil, Rnd., 4 oz.,
England, scarce,
(left side view) – **$40-53**

MEAD
(right side view)

Special Purpose Oilers

MICRO
Woodwind Oil, 1 oz.
(brown glass)
$7-12

Frank MILLER'S
Stop Squeak Spring Lubricant,
The Frank Miller Co., Rnd., 8
oz., circa 1920s-30s – **$24-33**

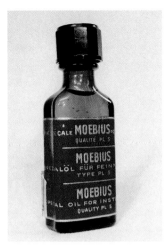

MOEBIUS
Special Oil for Instruments,
1 oz., (brown glass),
Switzerland – **$12-20**

OSTER OIL For Oster
Clippers & Electric Products,
John Oster Mfg. Co., Short,
Rect., 4 oz. – **$20-30**

PANEF
Electric Motor Oil,
Rect., 4 oz.
$13-18

PERFECTION
Pulsator Oil, Rect., 4 oz.,
circa 1950s-60s
$15-25

PHILLIPS Cycle
Lubricating Oil, J.A. Phillips
& Co., Ltd., Rect., 8 oz., with
3" spout, England – **$25-35**

REMINGTON
Shaver Lubricant,
1" wd. x 1/2" dp. x 13/4" tall,
glass bottle – **$5-10**

REMINGTON
Electric Shaver Service Kit,
Box= 31/2" wd. x 3/4" dp. x 3" tall,
(with oil, brush, & screwdriver) – **$10-18**

REVELATION For Slide
Trombones, S. Sternburg,
Chemist, Rnd., 2 oz.,
price 35 cents – **$9-16**

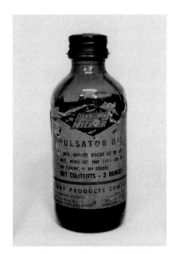

RITE-WAY MILKER
Pulsator Oil, Rnd., 3 oz.,
(brown glass) – **$10-14**

RITTER
Engine Oil, Rnd., 1 oz.,
circa 1959
$16-24

ROYAL
Rubber Lubricant,
Rect., 8 oz.
$9-13

RUNEESI
Cycle Lubricating Oil, Wide
Oval, 7 1/2 oz., soldered seams,
England, scarce – **$75+**

SCHICK Shaver Lubrication Kit,
Military Issue,circa WWI,
Pouch=4 1/2" wd. x 2 3/4" tall (with oil,
grease, brush & screwdriver) – **$12-23**

SCHWINN
Cycle Oil, Tall, Rect., 4 1/2 oz.,
circa 1963-73
$18-27

SCOTT & FETZER
Sanitation System Motor Oil,
Rnd., 1 1/2 oz., circa 1930s, price
25 cents, paper label – **$19-29**

SEARS
Electric Motor Oil, Rect.,
8 oz., circa 1963-73
$12-21

SEARS
Electric Motor Oil, Tall,
Rect., 4 oz.
$14-24

SEARS
Electric Pet Clipper Oil,
Rect., 4 oz.
$14-24

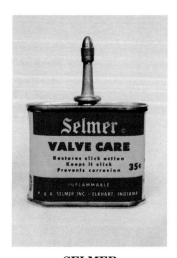

SELMER
Valve Care, H. & A. Selmer
Inc., Obl., 1 oz.,
price 35 cents – **$15-25**

SHIP – LOG OIL
Thomas Walker & Son, Ltd.,
3¹⁄₈" dia. x 4¹⁄₄" tall, England
$28-39

SKLAROL For Surgical
Apparatus & Pumps, J. Sklar
Mfg. Co., Oval, 3 oz.,
price 25 cents – **$28-38**

SPECIAL OIL For Motorized
Units, Minneapolis-Honeywell
Regulator Co., Short,
Rect., 4 oz. – **$19-29**

SPRING-EEZ
Halstead Specialties Co.,
Oval, 3 oz., copyright 1922,
very scarce – **$50-70**

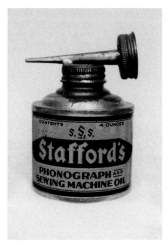

STAFFORD'S Phonograph
& Sewing Machine Oil, Rnd.,
4 oz., paper label, circa
1920s-30s – **$30-45**

STARRETT
Tool & Instrument Oil,
Oval, 4 oz., plastic
$10-15

STEWART Clipper Oil,
Chicago Flexible Shaft Co., 3"
dia. x 3¹⁄₄" tall (¹⁄₄ pint),
price 15 cents – **$38-52**

STURMEY-ARCHER
Cycle Oil, Raleigh Industries
Ltd., Rect., 8 oz., England
$28-38

SUMMIT
Lubricating Oil, (for cycles),
Rnd., 4 oz., New Zealand,
scarce – **$39-48**

SUPERB
Cycle Oil, Equitable Refining
Co., 2 oz., very scarce,
(front view) – **$45-60**

SUPERB
Cycle Oil, (close-up view)

SUPERIOR
Lubricating Oil for Cycles,
Wide, Oval, 7¹⁄₂ oz., England
$45-55

— SPECIAL PURPOSE OILERS —

SUPERIOR
Lubricating Oil for Cycles,
Rect., 8 oz., England
$39-49

SUPREME
Clipper Oil, Obl., 1 oz.
$17-25

TANKLESS
Air Compressors Motor Oil,
C.M. Sorensen Co., Rect., 4 oz.,
paper label – **$19-27**

THREE-IN-ONE
Cycle & Mower Oil, Rect.,
4-5 oz., England, (front view)
$29-42

THREE-IN-ONE
(back view)

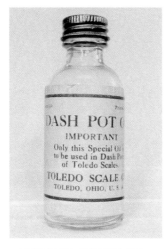

TOLEDO SCALE CO.
Dash Pot Oil, Rnd., 2 oz.
$12-19

TOP-NOTCH
Valve Oil, Top-Notch
Laboratory, 1 oz., price 25
cents – **$8-13**

TRU-ART
Modern Slide Oil, Oval,
1¹/₂ oz., price 25 cents
$29-39

V.B.P. Slicing Machine Oil,
Berkel Products Co., Ltd.,
Rnd., 4 oz., with 4¹/₂" spout,
Canada – **$25-35**

VELVET
Brake Compound, Mock &
Manuell, Rnd., 8 oz., paper
label, circa 1930s – **$20-30**

VERITY
Special Refrigeration Oil,
Wide Oval, 7¹/₂ oz., England
$25-32

WAHL
Hair Clipper Oil, Oval, 3 oz.,
(dark blue color)
$19-29

124

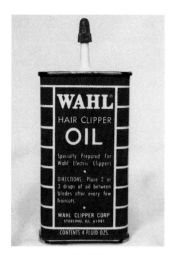

WAHL
Hair Clipper Oil, Rect., 4 oz.
$14-24

WAHL
Hair Clipper Oil, Rnd., 4 oz.
$2-4

WALTON
Motor Oil, (for Walton
Humidifiers) oval, 1 oz.,
paper label – **$20-30**

WESTERN ELECTRIC
Clothes Washer, Rnd., 3 oz.,
with 3" spout, circa 1930s,
very scarce – **$40-50**

SS. WHITE
Lubricating Oil, (for Dental
Equipment), Oval, 3 oz.
$35-45

SS. WHITE
Lubricating Oil, Rect., 4 oz.
$30-40